BUILD A HAPPIER BRAIN

The Neuroscience and Psychology of Happiness. Learn Simple Yet Effective Habits for Happiness in Personal, Professional Life and Relationships

SOM BATHLA

www.sombathla.com

Your Free Gift

As a token of my thanks for taking out time to read my book, I would like to offer you a free gift:

Click Below and Download your **Free Report**

Learn 5 Mental Shifts To Turbo-Charge Your Performance In Every Area Of Your Life - in Next 30 Days!

You can also grab your FREE GIFT Report through this below URL:

https://sombathla.lpages.co/5mentalshifts_bahb/

Table of Contents

Chapter 1: Introduction

****

"When I was five years old, my mother always told me that happiness was the key to life. When I went to school, they asked me what I wanted to be when I grew up. I wrote down 'happy'. They told me I didn't understand the assignment, and I told them they didn't understand life."

~John Lennon, Singer, Founder of Beatles

Happiness Requires a 'Shift' in Thinking

A group of around fifty people was attending a conference. Suddenly, the speaker stopped and decided to do a group activity; he gave each person a balloon. The participants were given a task to complete. Each one was asked to write his/her name on it using a marker pen.

Then all the balloons were collected and put in another room nearby. They were let in that room and asked to find the balloon which had their name written on it. They were given a time limit of five minutes to complete this exercise. Everyone frantically searched for their name, colliding with each other and pushing others, and there was utter chaos. At the end of five minutes, except for a few, no one could find the balloon with their name on it.

Next, the speaker modified the task slightly. This time, each one was asked to randomly collect a balloon and give it to the person whose name was written on it. Within minutes, everyone had their own balloon.

What can we learn from this story?

The moral of the story is: everyone is looking for happiness all around them, not knowing where it is. But if one becomes aware and shifts their attention to the right strategies and right factors to achieve happiness, it's within everyone's reach and way quicker than one thinks.

In our search for happiness, we are primarily looking at the external factors and believe that our happiness solely depends on them. But in reality, it's only when we redesign and rewire our brains differently, when we build happier brains, that happiness starts to surround us most of the time.

Before we begin building happier brains, let's see what a happier brain looks like.

Let's Look Inside the Happiest Brain

We all have seen happy people around us at times, though they are not plentiful these days.

How do they look? Often, they have a little smile on their faces, or sometimes a huge ear-to-ear smile; other times, they may chuckle or giggle or laugh heartily, often while playing with kids or having a great time with family and friends over dinner or drinks.

But happy, smiling faces are just output, and to only look at this output undermines the significance of internal programming that generates such kind of joyful output. There is much more going inside our brains to produce happiness that depends on our internal programming or the coding of our brain's software. Various types of chemical reactions inside our brains (more details on that later) create those feelings of joy and happiness.

When we are unaware of this internal coding, we mistakenly think that the relevant output is generated through some external factors. For example, you might think that happiness is generated solely because of having a large bank balance, luxurious house and cars, or delicious food. This is because happier faces and the external material things are both tangible. You can physically see them through your eyes and, therefore, on the surface, it appears that happiness is generated through these external factors. Yes, external factors add to happiness, but only in the short-term, and soon you look for more — they don't give you eternal happiness.

Do you want to see how does a happier brain looks on the inside?

Why not look inside the brain of a person who has been often referred to as the "happiest person in the world"?

Matthieu Ricard, a Buddhist monk with a French Ph.D. in molecular genetics and, eventually, the right-hand man for the Dalai Lama, had been the subject of intensive clinical tests at the University of Wisconsin; as a result of which he is frequently described[1] as the happiest man in the world. If you just Google "happiest person in the world" his name will pop up instantly.

The psychologist Dr. Daniel Goleman describes how a three-hour wait at an airport "sped by in minutes due to the sheer pleasure of Matthieu's

---

1 https://www.independent.co.uk/news/people/profiles/matthieu-ricard-meet-mr-happy-436652.html

orbit", as he exudes a sense of tranquillity, kindness and — surprisingly enough — humour.

In 2012, as part of his research, neuroscientist Richard Davidson, a professor of psychology and psychiatry at University of Wisconsin-Madison (and reported as one of the "The 100 Most Influential People in the world" by Time Magazine) and his team wired up the monk's skull with 256 sensors and conducted hours of continuous MRI scanning as a part of research study on hundreds of advanced practitioners of meditation about the impact of meditation on human brain[2].

The scans showed that when meditating, **Ricard's brain produces a level of gamma waves** — those linked to consciousness, attention, learning and memory — 'never reported before in the neuroscience literature', as per Neuroscientist Davidson. Gamma waves are associated with the **"feeling of blessings"** and create a state of peak concentration and high levels of cognitive functioning. Neuroscientists believe that gamma waves are able to link information from all parts of the brain.

Brain scans reveal that this French monk has an 'abnormally large capacity' for joy. The scans

[2] https://www.dailymail.co.uk/health/article-2225634/Is-worlds-happiest-man-Brain-scans-reveal-French-monk-abnormally-large-capacity-joy-meditation.html

showed excessive activity in his brain's left prefrontal cortex when compared to its right counterpart, giving him an **abnormally large capacity for happiness and a reduced propensity towards negativity.**

As you can see, the joy and happiness inside his brain didn't come from external factors; rather, it was all his inside programming through meditation and other lifestyle changes. Ricard attributes the reasons for his extreme levels of happiness to his deep meditation practices.

Practicing meditation plays a vital role in improving an individual's overall well-being. Ricard claims that after a regular practice of just one month, an individual will see benefits such as a reduction in the stress level and an increase in his/her general well-being.

But you and I don't need to turn into monks to experience an elevated level of joy. By understanding the psychology and neuroscience of happiness and implementing some simple habits, we can design a much happier brain that can empower us to experience higher dimensions and lead a quality life.

Why Do You Need a Happier Brain in Today's World?

A happier brain is a must for the overall well-being of any human being. There are huge benefits one can harness in many areas of life, be they personal, professional, relationship, etc. by understanding the psychology and neuroscience of happiness and implementing certain habits that work wonders, which we will understand in much greater detail in this book.

In his book *Happier,* Tal Ben-Shahar_describes "happiness" as the ultimate currency for human life. He states, *"A human being, like a business, earns profits and suffers losses. For a human being, however, the ultimate currency is not money, nor is it any external measure, such as fame, fortune, or power. The ultimate currency for a human being is happiness."*

In fact, across all the areas of our life, happiness generates numerous positive by-products that most of us have not yet taken time to understand. When we are happier, we do not only experience more joy, contentment, love, pride, and awe, but simultaneously, we also improve other aspects of our lives: our **energy levels**, our **immune systems**, our **engagement with work** and with other people, and our **physical and mental health**. We also strengthen our feelings of **self-confidence** and **self-esteem**; we start to believe that we are worthy, develop self-compassion, and feel deserving of respect.

In becoming happier, we not only **improve the quality of our lives**, but we also share the benefits of our happiness with our partners, families, communities, and even society at large.

Here is a quick list of the variety of benefits developing a happier brain offers to human beings:

- Improves heart rate
- Combats stress more effectively
- Creates a stronger immune system
- Creates an overall healthier lifestyle
- Reduces pain
- Increases life longevity
- Leads to better decision-making and problem-solving
- Improves individual and team productivity
- Better customer service abilities
- Helps you to be more productive, consequently earning more

Your Happiness is in Your Hands

"Happiness is not something ready-made. It comes from your own actions." ~ Dalai Lama

Happiness is nothing but an emotional state of pleasantness, just like other emotions of fear, anger, love, etc. The ultimate desire of any human being is to be in the state of constant pleasantness, and this desire prevails from the time he/she is born on this planet. No one ever wants to go through the pain, and everyone wants to have more and more feelings of pleasure.

Tony Robbins, the world-famous motivational speaker and performance strategist, states that all our behaviors and actions are influenced by two reasons, either to avoid the pain or enhance pleasure. Whatever you do in your life, the prime motivation behind that activity can't be anything else except to reduce your pain or enhance the levels of your happiness.

One could argue that all our technological developments are solely for the reason to alleviate our pain and enhances our pleasure. Medical science and the pharmaceutical industry were established to alleviate pain. All inventions, such as aeroplane, smartphone, or televisions, were created to improve our level of comfort or give us a more entertaining life experience.

The essential point here is that **we take action only to invite more happiness** into our lives. The quality or the direction of our actions might be flawed, and we might need some guidance, but achieving happiness is in our hands. Happiness is definitely a choice. It depends on the action or behavior we choose in our lives.

40% Rule of Happiness

Sonja Lyubomirsky, the author of *The How of Happiness,* suggests that we can significantly control the levels of our happiness based on the life values we adopt, our attitude or outlook towards the outside situation, and the habits we develop to automate certain kinds of behavior.

The "Happiness is a Stochastic Phenomenon" study, performed by David Lykken and Auke Tallegen of the University of Minnesota[3], shows that 50% of our happiness is dependent on our genetic makeup, and we can't change that.

Next is our life circumstances, such as education levels, marital status, wealth, etc.; these factors contribute merely an additional 10% to the level of our happiness. Money can reduce your physical pain, but it can't get you rid of your sadness. Money can definitely help you overcome all your physical discomforts and can put you in a more comfortable situation, but it can't help you get rid of mental discomfort.

The **remaining 40%** is about how you behave, act, and how you are influenced by outside circumstances. The essential thing to remember here is that 40% of the factors controlling your happiness are within your control. This means that you can start making changes in your life,

---

3 https://mctfr.psych.umn.edu/research/happiness.html

without blaming the outside world or your situations. Consequently, your happiness is in your hands. You need only to choose the best possible courses of action to get yourself moving in the right direction, and that's what the objective of this book is.

But You Have to Put in the Work

Everything that matters requires some work. To achieve anything substantial in life — learn a profession, master a sport, or raise a child, for example — a great amount of effort is required. But when it comes to mastering our mental or emotional lives, we find it difficult to apply similar principles. Without effort, we might get lucky sometimes, but that's not the best way to take control of your life.

You can't rely on luck solely, be it getting success in the outside material world, or winning your mind's game. Think about how much time, efforts and commitment many people devote to physical exercise, whether it's going to the gym, jogging, kickboxing, or yoga. Similarly, if you desire greater happiness, you will need to go about it in a similar way.

To put it simply, achieving lasting happiness requires making little difficult and permanent changes that require effort and commitment every day of your life. It takes work to pursue the journey of happiness, but consider that this happiness work may be the most rewarding work you'll ever do for a richer and rewarding life. Now, are you ready to jump inside the book?

Let me give you a quick introduction to what you'll find here.

What Will You Learn From This Book

The objective of this book is to teach you how to build a happier brain. It is my humble attempt to help you work towards the sometimes elusive state of mind called happiness. First, we'll go through the most common reasons for unhappiness. Then, we will examine the psychological aspects and various theories of happiness, as well as how neuroscience plays a role in generating happiness.

Finally, we will learn about personal, professional, and relational habits designed to make life happier and more fulfilling.

I hope you enjoy reading this book, and more importantly, implement some of the positive habits you find useful.

Let's get started and learn the most common reasons that most people are not happy today.

CHAPTER 1: KEY TAKEAWAYS

Happiness depends on what goes on inside your brain. If you learn to build a happier brain, this will not only **improve your physical and mental health**; you'll also attain more **financial success** and a **rewarding career**.

Happiness is your **life currency**, just like money is the currency for any business. Your primary objective should be to enhance your levels of happiness while pursuing your goals. Your happiness need not depend on outside events. You can **choose to create happiness** in your life, but you have to put in the work.

It demands making little difficult and permanent changes that require effort and commitment every day of your life. It **takes work to pursue the journey of happiness**, but consider that this happiness work may be the most rewarding work that you'll ever do for a richer and rewarding life.

Chapter 2: Most Common Reasons Why People Are Not Happy Today

****

"The primary cause of unhappiness is never the situation, but your thoughts about it."

~Eckhart Tolle

There was a little boy whose family was very wealthy. One day, his father took him on a trip to a poor country, as he wanted to show his son how poor people live. So, they arrived at the farm of a very poor family. They spent a few days there. On their return, the father asked his son if he liked the trip.

"Oh, it was great, dad!" the boy replied. "Did you notice how poor people live?" his father asked. "Yeah, I did," said the boy. The father asked his son to describe his impressions from their trip. Here is what the son responded: *"Well, we have only one dog, and they have many. In our garden, there is a pool, while they have a river that has no end. We've got expensive lanterns, but they have stars above their heads at night. We have the patio, and they have the whole horizon. We have only a small piece of land, while they have endless fields. We buy food, but they grow it. We have a high fence for protection of our property, and they don't need it, as their friends protect them."*

The father was stunned. He could not say a word. Then the boy added: "Thank you, Dad, for letting me see how poor we are." This story shows that true happiness cannot be measured solely by the parameters of material wealth. Love, friendship and freedom play a vital role in generating happiness.

Let me clarify; I'm not against earning big money and striving to obtain the life that you dream of. But here is the key thing. Of course, money can buy things that generate happiness. You get good food, good clothes, a big house, a big car, and you name it, money can buy everything for you, but the problem arises when you think that money is the sole contributor to happiness.

In fact, a study[4] was conducted in 2010 at Princeton University to assess the influence of income on happiness. The results were

[4] http://wws.princeton.edu/news-and-events/news/item/two-wws-professors-release-new-study-income%E2%80%99s-influence-happiness

surprising, as the study showed that an annual income of up to $75,000 was considered a benchmark for happiness. The lower a person's annual income falls below that benchmark, the unhappier he or she feels. But whatever more money they make beyond that benchmark of $75,000 doesn't provide more happiness in the same proportion.

This study is around a decade old (and maybe the numbers might have slightly increased), but the point is that beyond a certain level of income, money does not increase an individual's happiness in the same proportion.

Money provides happiness when having it means that you don't have to struggle for your basic necessities. The modern data[5] from the world happiness index shows that the first world countries as a whole stand higher in ranking in the happiness index, as compared to the third world countries.

But we are talking about **individual happiness**. We are talking about yours and my happiness, and therefore, taking an average of the millions of people living in one particular country is not something you would want to rely

---

[5] https://countryeconomy.com/demography/world-happiness-index and https://en.wikipedia.org/wiki/World_Happiness_Report

on heavily when it comes to your own personal level of happiness.

You might be living in a poor country, but with a happier brain, you can still lead a life of joy and abundance. Or someone might be living in the richest country in the world, but due to lack of a resourceful brain, he or she might end up living a life of disappointment and misery.

In this chapter, we will analyze the most common reasons why people are unhappy in today's world. This by no means is an exhaustive list of reasons, as there are billions of people with different backgrounds, life experiences, and many other circumstances, so there can't be a comprehensive list. You may have some of your own reasons, but generally, they will fit somehow in, or maybe closer to the most common reasons listed below.

Needless Comparison with Others without Knowing Their Journey

Each time we see someone more successful and famous than us, we often think, "Wow. Some people have it all. I really wish that my life was like that! My life has so many problems." And then we make a list of what we lack and what the other person has, be it better relationships, a better career, or more material possessions. We forget something very important — we are comparing our 'entire' life with another individual's summary of life achievements, which shows only the good, jazzy and exciting stuff. We don't pay attention to the struggles the individual must have gone through to get a certain level of success.

The success we see is the tip of the iceberg. We see the good life someone leads and assume he/she received everything on a silver platter. Little do we know about the difficult times the individual must have gone through to reach a certain level of success.

We see the person winning the gold medal in the Olympics, and we never stop to think about all of the hard work that they put in to achieve that goal. We do not reflect upon the arduous process of years of hard training and days and nights of shedding sweat and tears to win that prestigious award for an outstanding performance for just a few seconds or minutes.

Daley Thompson, the famous British athlete, who won the Gold medal in the Decathlon event in both the 1980 Moscow Olympics and the 1984 Los Angeles Olympics, played a major role in re-defining the training manual for athletes.

Let me ask you about the first thoughts that come to your mind when the word Christmas is mentioned. Certainly, almost everyone thinks of celebrations with family and friends, or maybe the loads of goodies and gifts that we receive. Would you like to hazard a guess about Daley

Thompson's routine on this day? Well, he trained full steam on Christmas in order to gain an edge over his opponents! Not only that, he set in motion a culture where a whole new generation of athletes and coaches now consider Christmas Day training to be perfectly normal.

More often than not, in today's uber-competitive sporting world, where the margin between victory and defeat is razor-thin, every extra hour, even every minute of training could make the difference between victory and defeat.

Here's the proof: In the Men's 100-metre final in the 2016 Olympics[6] in Rio de Janeiro, the legendary Usain Bolt won the gold medal in just 9.81 seconds. Travyon Bromell, the man who finished last (or eighth), clocked 10.06 seconds! The difference between the winner and the man who finished last was a mere 0.25 seconds.

Who said that success comes easy? Was success handed on a silver platter to Daley Thompson? Travyon Bromell finished last in the 2016 Olympics 100-metre final. But was he lazy? Did he not train hard? Ask yourself: What lessons can we draw from the above examples? What we see is the ultimate success, not the effort and heartbreaks along the path to success. There is a price to pay for success, and if you compare your

---

[6] https://www.bbc.com/sport/olympics/rio-2016/results/sports/athletics/mens-100m

life with that of others without knowing and being willing to pay the price they paid for, this itself is the recipe for unhappiness.

The Artificial Persona You Maintain in the Online World

In today's digital age, people are constantly exposed to what others display on social media. Earlier, before the onslaught of social media, we compared our possessions in the offline world, such as cars and homes and bank balances with others, especially family and friends. Now, not only do we compare our social lives and possessions with our family and friends, as well as celebrities and the rich and the famous, but there's a completely new dimension to this. You can call it '*maintaining an online persona*.' This online persona is meant to just show off to these so-called 'online friends,' who are often just that, "online friends."

More often than not, most of them have little or no connection with us in the real world. And the criteria by which so many of us compare ourselves with others could be something as arbitrary as the number of likes we've obtained on an uploaded photo versus the number of likes one of our online friends may have obtained. Here is how that affects us: to get that perfect picture on vacation to upload on social media, we completely forget to be in the moment.

With the virtual world just a click away, we have taken the art of comparing the lives we lead to a dangerously new level!

> ***"Did you ever see an unhappy horse? Did you ever see a bird that had the blues? One reason why birds and horses are not unhappy is because they are not trying to impress other birds and horses."***
>
> ***– Dale Carnegie***

I remember talking to one of my friends, who admitted that she didn't feel good when any of her posts got less than 100 likes; she coped with this by refreshing her posts repeatedly every few minutes. Another friend once asked me why didn't I see and like her photos. I felt unable to admit to her how I felt: If I didn't like her images, why should I 'like' them?

When we depend on others in order to feel good, especially on social media, we hand control of our lives over to other people, and only when they press a (like) button will we become happier.

Association with Negative People

We are known by the company we keep. If we surround ourselves with positive people, their positivity will rub off on us. As Jim Rohn said, *"You are the average of the five people you spend the most time with"*. On the other hand, if we seek out negative people, the opposite holds true. Complainers are exactly that: energy vampires. They constantly focus on all the negative in the world, be it in people or the general environment. They need an excuse to crib. They re-enforce all the negative occurrences that are taking place by complaining and cribbing constantly.

I am not saying that we shouldn't lend a sympathetic ear to people when they go through a low phase. It's good to be compassionate, yet, at the same time, it is imperative that we set our boundaries. It is one thing to be sympathetic and helpful to someone who's going through a low phase. It is another thing altogether to listen to negative people who complain all the time.

If a car or truck is emitting poisonous exhaust fumes, you would not just sit there and inhale those fumes, right? You would move away, and you should do the same with chronic complainers.

Not Letting Go of the Past

Does your mind often wander back to the past, especially unpleasant incidents? Here's the result. You hold grudges and waste precious energy that could be utilized effectively in more productive and positive endeavors. Holding a grudge or grouse can be compared to drinking poison and expecting the other person to die. Being stuck in the past does nobody any good, least of all you, and builds up toxic emotions. In the end, you end up harming yourself and nobody else. For your own sake, let go of all the bitterness and resentment. Forgiveness is a sign of strength and maturity, not weakness.

Lack of Family and Friends

Human beings, by nature, have a need to seek out and maintain meaningful relationships. If we isolate ourselves and do not have family and friends that we can turn to, then the lack of social relationships can be among the biggest drivers of unhappiness. We all need people who we are close to, to whom we can pour our hearts out, who can be there for each other, and with whom we can do things together. The more self-absorbed we are, the narrower our perspective and vision are.

Studies have shown that remaining in isolation and having fewer social connections leads to unhappiness. Numerous studies have looked at the connection between social connection and well-being, and all find that the one predicts the other. One of the most famous, a Harvard study[7] that followed people for a long period of 80 years, found that people with stronger social connections were the healthiest and happiest. Social connectivity over a lifetime was the key variable that predicted happiness and longevity.

Seeing the World through Your Own Narrow Prism

Let us be realistic here. Life can be unfair, and on numerous occasions, it can seem unjustifiably so. Your opinion may mean the world to you, and your lofty ideals might seem the perfect manual to conduct worldly affairs.

Well, the reality is quite different. One, people will often disagree with your deeply ingrained beliefs, value system and ideas. Remember, they, too, have their own deeply ingrained beliefs, value system and ideas. It doesn't matter who's right and who's wrong. Remember, the very people you expect to conform to your belief system and ideas are expecting the same from you, as well as others. Many of them are feeling

---

7 https://news.harvard.edu/gazette/story/2017/04/over-nearly-80-years-harvard-study-has-been-showing-how-to-live-a-healthy-and-happy-life/

as frustrated and angry as you are, and sometimes even more so because the world does not conform to the prism through which 'they' view it. Each time we feel anger and frustration when the world does not conform to our values and ideas, remember that it takes all kinds of people to make up this world.

One of the world's best-known skeptics and critical thinkers, Michael Shermer, author of *The Believing Brain*, has rightly stated the reasoning of why people believe anything at all. He bluntly puts it this way:

"We form our beliefs for a variety of subjective, personal, emotional, and psychological reasons in the context of environments created by family, friends, colleagues, culture, and society at large; after forming our beliefs, we then defend, justify, and rationalize them with a host of intellectual reasons, cogent arguments, and rational explanations. Beliefs come first; explanations for beliefs follow."

Lack of Gratitude

We should always remember that we cannot have everything in life. And, in fact, we don't even need everything to be happy in life either. Often, it is the lack of simplicity which prevents us from feeling grateful for all the things we already have been blessed with. We can be grateful for something as simple as waking up this morning. After all, many people did not wake up alive today! It is a human tendency to take the most basic things in life for granted; these things are often the most important.

Our laundry list of what we want from life is a never-ending pit, which, time and again, tends to spiral out of control. Examples are a more expensive car, a bigger house, and designer clothing, to name just a few. We keep running after things that do not necessarily translate into more happiness.

Again, let me be very clear here. I am not against material success in life; rather, I'm all for it. But my philosophy is not to acquire material possessions for their own sake. Money is a form of value exchange. So, work to earn money to become the kind of person who can generate that value. Use money as a metric to measure the value you provide to the world.

Moreover, the journey of your life should be perused with two simultaneous lenses. You should look at what you have and be grateful because most people on the planet haven't even got that. I don't know your personal income is, but still, I guarantee that most people who are reading this book are in the top 95% of the population in terms of their wealth.

Check it out for yourself; just go to the website http://www.globalrichlist.com. Insert your annual income, and it will tell you where you stand in terms of your income. If you have a job or run a small business with a reasonable income, there is a strong chance that you'll land in the top 5% (or maybe the top 1%) of the world population from a material wealth perspective. That means you are way better off than 95% of the world population.

So, you should be grateful for all that you have. If you have got good health, a healthy family and reasonable money to live happily, you are already more blessed than 95% of the world's population. But being grateful for what you have doesn't equate to being complacent and not taking any steps towards improving your life. Being grateful doesn't mean to become lethargic and lazy, not growth-oriented. While being grateful, you have to be exploring your untapped potential and grow. As you will learn in a later chapter, that growth is one of the most important needs of human being's fulfilment.

We will learn later in the book about how to build your gratitude muscles with practice.

What's the Level of Your Happiness?

Do you want to know how happy you are? Do you want to test your levels of happiness?

Martin Seligman, known as the father of positive psychology (along with researchers from the University of Pennsylvania) have created a few tests to measure the level of your happiness in general. These scales will show the level of your happiness compared to the other people in your age group, gender, education level, location, etc.

You can check your general Happiness Scale by clicking on this link. You just need to sign up (it's free) with Penn University to take these tests:

https://www.authentichappiness.sas.upenn.edu/questionnaires/general-happiness-scale

Also, if you want to do a happiness inventory of how you have been feeling for the entire past week, here is what you can get an assessment of your happiness inventory.

https://www.authentichappiness.sas.upenn.edu/questionnaires/authentic-happiness-inventory

I hope you'll get good happiness scores. Please go ahead and do your assessment; I'll wait for you here, and then we will proceed to the next chapter, where we will go deeper into the human psychology of happiness and the popular theories which surround it.

CHAPTER 2: KEY TAKEAWAYS

Of course, money plays a significant role in bringing happiness into your life; but you commit a big mistake when you attribute money as a sole factor to happiness. Other than a lack of money, there are many reasons why most people are not happy today. Here are some of the most common reasons.

- **Needless comparison** with others without knowing their journey: If you are not willing to pay the price what others have paid, don't compare; you'll only invite unhappiness.

- Maintaining an **artificial online persona**: Living an inauthentic life will bring you more stress.

- Association with **negative people**: They suck all the energy and happiness out of you.

- Continuously **regretting your past**: You can't drive your car fast if you keep looking in the rear-view mirror.

- **Lack of family and friends**: Humans are designed to thrive in communities with others. Social isolation can also cause illness.

- Seeing the world through your **own narrow prism**: No man is an island; expand your horizon by understanding others' perspectives.

- **Lack of gratitude**: If you are not grateful for what you have, what's the probability of becoming happier when you get more? Savour what you have while striving for what you want.

Chapter 3: How the Psychology of Happiness Works

****

"Very little is needed to make a happy life. It is all within YOURSELF in your way of thinking.

~ Marcus Aurelius

People in the United States and in most of the world loved this person. He started his career as a stand-up comedian in San Francisco and Los Angeles in the mid-1970s and established himself as a success icon through his leading show, *San Francisco's Comedy Renaissance*. He rose to the pinnacle of his fame through his comedy show, *Mork and Mindy*.

And he didn't simply stop at comedy; he also challenged himself to win an Academy Award by acting in films. He won the 1997 Academy Award, and besides that, during the course of his entire career, he won two Emmy Awards, seven Golden Globe Awards, and four Grammy Awards, to list a few[8].

[8] https://en.wikipedia.org/wiki/Robin_Williams

Yes, I am talking about Robin Williams, the comedy star. By all measures, this man was accomplished; wherever he put his hands, he emerged as a successful man — be it television or films, he left his own mark in the industry. He was a master of the science of achievement. But, surprisingly, he ended his life by hanging himself in his home in 2014, an event that shook the entire world.

Tony Robbins said, in one of his videos[9] that in all his events across the world, be it Australia, Beijing, Tokyo, United States, or Brazil, upon being asked whether people loved Robin Williams, 98-99% people raised their hands. He had tens of millions of fans in the world who cherished the joy spread by Robin Williams. Then Tony made one touching statement: "This man (Williams) made the whole world laugh with joy, except himself."

Despite having all the worldly pleasures that one could dream of and huge success in life, Williams ended dying of depression; he took his own life. He was undoubtedly very successful, but the way he ended his life demonstrates that his success couldn't give his life meaning or fulfillment.

---

[9] https://www.inc.com/video/tony-robbins-why-success-without-fulfilllment-is-the-ultimate-failure.html

Different views have been expressed by people around the world about his committing suicide, some stating that he took such a drastic step under the influence of his severe depression and mental illness. On the other hand, people like Tony Robbins, while praising Williams for being a good man, unquestionably adored by the whole world, state that Williams had to end his life because he couldn't find enough fulfilment in his success to finally lead a happy life.

Without getting much into any controversy about the reasons for his ending his life, the message that one can draw out of the above life story is that material success does not guarantee fulfillment or meaning in one's life.

We've talked a lot, up until this point, about what doesn't lead to happiness. Now, let's start exploring the factors that lead to **genuine happiness** in our lives. In this chapter, we will go through some psychological theories about happiness to understand how the evolution of these theories can help us understand different parameters of happiness.

You might ask: Why do we need to look at psychological studies on happiness? Why not directly get into the happiness how-tos?

It's because our logical mind often gets in the way of the implementation of some practices if we don't convince ourselves with the rationale or logical arguments behind anything. We can better focus and implement the how-tos when we have a logical understanding of the rationale behind different approaches.

Psychology, as a subject matter, is nothing but a **scientific study of the human mind and its functions,** especially those affecting behavior in a given context. So, let's get started with some background.

In fact, man has pondered how to achieve happiness since the beginning of time. Happiness has been the topic of discussion since the Ancient Greek period. There have been two broad aspects or concepts of happiness. They are **Hedonia** (a Greek word meaning 'a condition of pleasure' or cheerfulness) and **Eudaimonia** (a Greek word meaning 'human flourishing or prosperity': a sense that life is well-lived).

Aristippus, a Greek philosopher from the 4th century BC, claimed that happiness was the sum of life's hedonic moments. Hedonic enjoyment is a state whereby an individual feels relaxed, has a **sense of distance from their problems**, and can be said to feel 'happy' (Ryan & Deci, 2001). Hedonism advocates that a **happy life is all about maximized emotions of pleasure** and minimized pain. A happy person is very cheerful and smiles a lot, with many intense episodes of pleasure and very few episodes of pain.

On the other hand, another Greek philosopher, **Aristotle**, argued that because of man's unique capacity to reason, pleasure alone could not achieve happiness — because animals are driven to seek pleasure, and man has greater capacity than animals. Eudaimonic theories of happiness argue that rather than the pursuit of pleasure, happiness is the result of the development of individual strengths and virtues. In striving for happiness, the most important factor is for a person to have 'complete virtue' — in other words, to have good moral character. Eudaimonia was, according to Aristotle, "**activity expressing virtue**" that will, therefore, lead to a happy life.

Therefore, happiness encompasses two inseparable aspects: hedonia (pleasure of the senses and positive affect) and eudaimonia (pleasure of reason: living well and doing well, cognitive appraisals of meaning and life satisfaction).

During our times, or what we define as modern history, there has been in-depth research, study and analysis of the psychology of happiness. This has led to the development of a variety of scientific theories of happiness. As a matter of fact, these different theories of happiness have undergone a transformation over the past few years.

Sigmund Freud, an Austrian neurologist, propounded the concept of psychoanalysis. Psychoanalysis places emphasis on unconscious conflict and childhood traumas and their impact on the development of later personality traits and psychological problems. The goal of psychoanalysis is to bring what exists at the unconscious or subconscious level up to consciousness and is commonly used to treat depression and anxiety disorders.

At the beginning of the 20th century, psychological research was focused primarily on mental illness; the researchers were trying to understand depression, schizophrenia, and other negative aspects of human behavior. This continued until the concept of positive psychology was introduced by Martin Seligman, also known as the 'Father of Positive Psychology,' who is the most renowned advocate of positive psychology. As the President of the American Psychological Association, he went against psychology's emphasis on scarcity and sickness. In fact, in positive psychology, he underlined the equal significance of helping people flourish above the norm and coined the term "Positive".

Precisely, the previous focus on mental illness enabled humans to take someone from -9 to -3 to 0 through psychotherapy, but as per Seligman, it was time to take someone from 0 to +3 to +9. This was a **major shift from the**

concept of mental illness to focusing on improving mental health.

I don't want to bombard you with tons of psychological background and theories; I want to stick only to what is necessary for you to understand the concept better. This is because I have got feedback from my readers that they prefer my books because of my optimal synthesis of the relevant information and how I present them useful chunks of helpful advice. However, I also appreciate that some of the readers do like to go much more deeply into the background and detailed theories related to the subject, and for such readers, the footnotes can help them to delve as deeply into the subject as they want.

Therefore, let's briefly talk about Martin Seligman's approach to attaining authentic happiness and how finally he concluded his theory of human well-being.

Authentic Happiness to Well Being

In his 2002 book, *Authentic Happiness,* Martin Seligman said that there are **three distinct orientations** of happiness, namely: (1) the **Pleasant** Life or pleasures, (2) the **Good** Life or engagement, and (3) the **Meaningful** Life. While the first two criteria are subjective in nature, the third is at least partly objective and examines what is more meaningful than merely catering to the self's pleasures and desires.

While the three orientations of happiness was a decent theory, in less than ten years, in 2011, Seligman gave the short shrift to the three orientations to happiness and revealed his **new model**, known as PERMA, which added two new dimensions to the earlier three orientations of happiness: namely, Accomplishment and Positive Relationships.

PERMA is also known as **the well-being theory**, with well-being, and not happiness, being the key focus of positive psychology, whereas, in the authentic happiness theory, happiness is the key focus area.

The theory comprises five core elements, with each playing a role in well-being:

P- Positive Emotions: It's about feeling good, about optimism, pleasure and enjoyment.

E- Engagement: This is based on the premise that happiness arises from fulfilling work, interesting hobbies, and flow.

R- Relationships: Social connections, love, intimacy, and emotional and physical connection increase happiness.

M- Meaning: Having a purpose, finding meaning in life is an important factor.

A- Accomplishments: Ambitions, realistic goals, important achievements, and pride in yourself contribute to contentment.

One must strive to meet the requirements of all five elements of PERMA to achieve the optimal state of well-being. Let's go through each of them in a bit more detail.

P: Positive Emotions

Life satisfaction and happiness are important aspects of this element. This factor has, in all probability, the most evident correlation with happiness. To focus one's attention on positive emotions goes beyond a mere smile — it is the **ability to retain an optimistic outlook and view one's past, present, and future with a positive outlook.**

An optimistic attitude improves personal and professional relationships and fosters creative thinking and risk-taking. In addition to this, there are many health benefits that result from optimism and positivity, including a strengthened immune system and good mental health. Conversely, if one has a negative attitude, due to unpleasant past experiences or a less than ideal current situation, there is an increased likelihood that one might develop depression.

What is the difference between pleasure and enjoyment in this context? **Pleasure** deals with gratifying physical needs for survival, which include thirst, hunger, and sleep. On the other hand, **enjoyment** is a result of intellectual stimulation and creative thinking.

For example, when one completes a crossword or a Sudoku puzzle, it can be a source of immense pleasure because it requires focus and application and gives one a sense of accomplishment. This is vital, as it can help people persist with challenges that they face by helping them to retain a positive outlook.

E: Engagement

Here, a person always looks to engage in activities that elevate one's sense of well-being and allow one to be in a state of flow or profound, natural involvement. This occurs primarily when we focus on activities that moderately challenge our intelligence, skills, and emotional capabilities.

People find enjoyment in different things, whether it's playing an instrument, playing a sport, dancing, working on an interesting project at work, or even just participating in a hobby. When **time truly "flies by" during an activity**, it is likely because the people involved are experiencing this sense of engagement.

We all need something in our lives that causes us to be engaged in the current moment, creating a '**flow**' of blissful immersion into the task or activity. This 'flow' of engagement stretches our intelligence, skills, and **emotional capabilities**. Such activities help us to experience calm, focus, and joy and include playing a sport, a hobby, or an interesting professional project. Seligman recommends that in order to achieve this, we must recognize our key strengths and learn how to practice them.

If you want to test your basic strengths, you can undergo a free assessment questionnaire by the University of Pennsylvania on this link:
https://www.authentichappiness.sas.upenn.edu/questionnaires/brief-strengths-test

This engagement aspect of the PERMA model was also researched in detail by another psychologist, the co-founder of positive psychology Mihaly Csikszentmihalyi, and he named it 'Flow'. He states: *"The best moments in our lives are not the passive, receptive, relaxing times. The best moments usually occur if a person's body or mind is stretched to its limits in a voluntary effort to accomplish something difficult and worthwhile."*

Csikszentmihalyi wrote the book *Flow: The Psychology of Optimal Experience*, wherein he concluded that happiness is an internal state of being and not an external one. In this book, he mentions that one's **happiness level can be significantly enhanced by introducing flow** into whatever we do.

Csikszentmihalyi described eight characteristics of someone who is in the state of flow:

- Complete concentration on the task
- Clarity of goals, keeping the reward in mind, and immediate feedback
- Transformation of time (speeding up/slowing down)
- Experience is intrinsically rewarding
- Effortlessness and ease
- Balance between challenge and skills
- Merged actions and awareness; loss of self-conscious rumination
- Feeling of control over the task

To achieve a state of flow, one needs to get rid of all kinds of distractions. Also, the balance of perceived challenges and skills is important to flow. When a challenge is greater than one's level of skill, one becomes anxious and stressed. On the other hand, when the level of skill exceeds the size of the challenge, one becomes bored and distracted. Csikszentmihalyi concluded that "Inducing flow is about the balance between the level of skill and the size of the challenge at hand".

R: Relationships

Relationships and social bonds are critical for us and help us to sustain the other four elements of well-being. Humans flourish through relationships that encourage love and closeness, as well as a strong emotional connection and physical interaction with other humans, especially one's immediate family members, colleagues and friends, and provide crucial support in turbulent times.

In an interview with Dr. Mitch Prinstein, a Professor of Psychology and Neuroscience at the University of North Carolina, he discussed the research on pain centers in the human brain. Basically, our **brain's pain centers become activated when we are at risk of isolation**. From an evolutionary perspective, self-isolation is the worst thing we can do for survival. These activation centers are like fire alarms in the body, discouraging people from continuing feeling this pain, and ideally, reconnect socially with someone or a group. We need, neurologically, to know that we belong to a group; it helps us feel safe and valued and has for millions of years.[10]

Seligman once said, *"Is there someone in your life whom you would feel comfortable phoning*

---

[10] https://positivepsychologyprogram.com/perma-model/

at four in the morning to tell your troubles to? If your answer is yes, you will likely live longer than someone whose answer is no."

M: Meaning

A person with a meaningful life has a sense of belonging and affinity towards, as well as serves, something/someone beyond just his own self, such as family and friends, religion, and country, among others. Apart from religion and spirituality, other avenues that endow people's lives with meaning include voluntary and charitable work, raising children, and creative expression.

Precisely, living a meaningful life is related to attaching oneself to something larger than oneself. This instils the sense that there is a larger purpose to one's life, being a part of this larger entity confers meaning. Having such connections is also an effective barrier against depression.

Victor Frankl, an Austrian neurologist and psychiatrist, in his great book *Man's Search for Meaning,* said:

"Don't aim at success—the more you aim at it and make it a target, the more you are going to miss it. For success, like happiness, cannot be

pursued; it must ensue, and it only does so as the ***unintended side effect of one's personal dedication to a cause greater than oneself or as the by-product of one's surrender to a person other than oneself****. Happiness must happen, and the same holds for success: you have to let it happen by not caring about it.*

A: Accomplishments

To give life direction and to achieve an inner sense of accomplishment, we need goals and aspirations. The key is to set realistic, achievable goals. Just making the effort to attain those goals can bestow upon us a sense of satisfaction. And once we finally realize those goals, we feel a sense of pride and achievement.

Success, winning, achievement and mastery, are end-goals and processes for achieving that state of accomplishment. Seligman also states that many people would chase accomplishment for the sake of it, even though they are devoid of positive emotions or meaning.

To conclude, PERMA, or the **well-being theory**, is broad in both method and substance.

Positive emotion is a subjective variable, characterized by our thoughts and feelings. Meaning, relationships, and accomplishment have subjective, as well as objective constituents. We might think that we possess meaning, great relationships, and first-rate accomplishments in our lives and be completely off the mark.

The positive side of this model is that well-being cannot just be concocted. Well-being is an amalgamation of both feeling good (subjective), along with meaning, good relationships, and accomplishment (objective). The key is to maximize the application of all of the five components in the PERMA model.

CHAPTER 3: KEY TAKEAWAYS

Success without fulfillment is the ultimate failure.

There are two broad aspects or concepts of happiness: **Hedonia** (i.e. all about maximized emotions of pleasure and minimized pain) and **Eudaimonia** (i.e. happiness is a result of the development and expression of individual strengths and virtues).

Instead of focusing solely on the pleasures of life, we need to also focus on leaving a life of meaning.

Martin Seligman, also known as the father of positive psychology, over a period of time, developed certain theories around happiness and finally concluded with the '**Well-being Theory**" or **PERMA Model**. PERMA is an acronym where each letter describes a factor that plays a vital role in human well-being. It is composed of:

> **P**- Positive Emotions: Feeling good, optimism, pleasure and enjoyment
>
> **E**- Engagement: Fulfilling work, interesting hobbies, and flow
>
> **R**- Relationship: Social connection, love, intimacy, emotional and physical connection

M- Meaning: Having a purpose, finding meaning in life

A- Accomplishments: Ambitions, realistic goals, important achievements, pride in yourself

All the elements of the PERMA model play a vital role, and you can significantly improve your life's well-being by focusing on and taking care of all the elements together.

Chapter 4: The Key Drivers of Happiness & Fulfillment

****

"Your long-term happiness and fulfillment depend on your ability to fulfill your soul's unique purpose and to fill the place in the world that only you can fill, making the contribution that only you can make."

~ Rod Stryker

Have we ever thought about why we act in a certain way? What are the inspirations behind our feelings, actions, standards of living and eventual destinies? What are the key drivers that guide our actions in our quest to attain a state of happiness?

The moment a human being is born, desires occur within him. While in infancy, our primary needs are physiological; as we grow up, psychological needs start to become extremely significant. These desires, when met, give us an immediate sense of happiness and joy, but then a new set of desires starts to take place.

In this chapter, we will look at the psychology of human needs and how they affect our actions or behaviors.

I. Hierarchy of Human Needs

Abraham Maslow, an American psychologist, researched the different needs of human beings and gave them a hierarchy in proportion to the growth aspects of human life. His theory is famously known as Maslow's hierarchy of human needs.

The pyramid below explains his explanation of various types of needs:

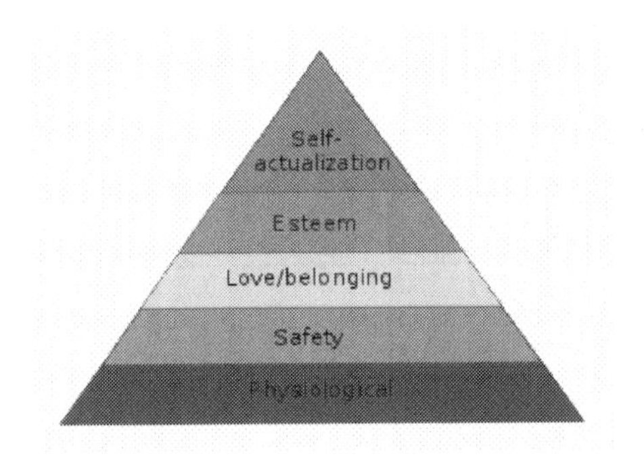

(Image courtesy: Wikipedia)

Maslow explained as part of his initial study that there are five kinds of human needs, and they start from the lowest end of the pyramid. However, in the latter part of his career, Maslow discovered that these five needs are related to human's own needs, and he introduced the sixth need of humans. The Maslow Hierarchy of needs theory paper that was submitted in 1943 covered these five needs.

Here's what these needs are:

- **Physiological**: These needs are limited to the survival of humans and are most important for the survival of the human body. They include water, food, clothing, shelter, breathing, sex, etc.

- **Safety**: Once the physiological needs of a person are reasonably satisfied, the needs for safety and security govern his behavior. Safety includes safety from war, natural disaster, economic safety, health-related safety, i.e. access to healthcare if needed.

- **Love & Belonging**: After physiological and safety needs are fulfilled, the third level of human needs is interpersonal and involves feelings of belongingness. It includes the need for family, friends, and an intimate relationship with someone.

- **Esteem:** Esteem needs are ego needs or status needs, such as recognition, status, importance, and respect from others. All humans have a need to feel respected; this includes the need to have self-esteem and self-respect.

- **Self-Actualization**: This level of need refers to what a person's full potential is and the realization of that potential. Maslow describes this level as the desire to accomplish everything that one can, to become the most one can be.

But Victor Frankl, who wrote *The Man's Search for Meaning* after his torturous stay in Germany's concentration camps during World War II, thought the entire focus on oneself was narcissistic and ultimately detrimental. He suggested real fulfillment in life occurs only when a person transcends the self.

In the latter part of his career, Maslow understood the importance of Frankl's words. Influenced by Frankl's work, he explored a further dimension of needs in 1969 while criticizing his own vision on self-actualization. He propounded the sixth need: self-transcendence.

- **Self-Transcendence**: The need for self-transcendence states that the self only finds its actualization in giving itself to some higher outside goal. He said, *"The fully developed (and very fortunate) human being working under the best conditions tends to be motivated by values which transcend his self. They are not selfish any more in the old sense of that term*[11]*."*

You can see that your parent's lives, and your life, follow the above pattern of needs. If you started your life at the lower rungs of the pyramid, you can easily relate to those stages of your life and the prioritization of your needs.

You must have started with caring about your basic needs of food, shelter; before moving to your personal safety needs. Once your physiological and safety needs were met, then you'd have moved to love and belonging and then to the need for self-esteem. If you are growth-minded, then you are already on the path of actualizing your full potential by way of learning new skills and implementing in your chosen pursuits.

---

[11] A. H. Maslow, "The Farther Reaches of Human Nature," Journal of Transpersonal Psychology 1, no. 1 (1969): 1–9.

But the point here is that the first five needs are related to your own self-needs, and once you reach the apex of your five-step pyramid, you will still lack fulfillment. It's your craving to contribute to the world that transcends beyond yourself which ultimately gives you a sense of fulfillment.

In the previous chapter, we learned about the PERMA model, and the constituent 'meaning' also has a similar connotation of finding a purpose or meaning in life that transcends from one's self.

II. Inherent Psychological Needs:

Edward L. Deci and Richard M. Ryan, psychologists at the University of Rochester, propounded a theory of motivation and personality famously known as **self-determination theory**. This theory states that humans are motivated to grow and evolve by the satisfaction of their inherent psychological needs.

This theory essentially identifies **three native and universal key psychological needs.**

Only once the basic physical needs (of food, clothing and shelter) are met can we deal with the psychological ones. Here are the three key psychological needs, as propounded by Self-Determination Theory.

- **The Need for Connection**: One study that examined 10% of the happiest people of the world found that they have at least one intimate relationship. Therefore, it was stated that a sense of belongingness or intimate connection is not a luxury; rather, it is a necessity to be a part of the happiest group.

- **The Need for Mastery**: The next psychological requirement is his need to be efficacious in whatever he or she chooses as a career. This need is for attaining mastery in one's chosen field of activity. We need to feel that we are good at something, i.e., our profession or hobbies, etc. If you don't feel that you are good at something, then you won't be truly happy, and chances are, you won't be able to earn big money.

- **The Need for a Sense of Autonomy**: The last need is the need not to be controlled by anyone and to be able to make decisions independently. That's the reason we want to resist situations where we don't have the freedom to do whatever we wish. Therefore, the desire for autonomy is wired into our brains, like the desire for connection and mastery.

III. The Six Core Human Needs for Fulfilment

Tony Robbins, a leading life and business strategist, has deeply analyzed human behavior and motivation for over four decades and concluded that there are six human needs that primarily influence our behavior and choices. Each individual ranks these needs differently, resulting in different decisions, based upon which needs we rank highest. We fulfil these needs continuously, either in beneficial, neutral or detrimental ways.

Robbins combined his findings with Neural Linguistic Programming (NLP), Cognitive Therapy, and several other theories, along with Maslow's Hierarchy of Needs. He thus developed **a dynamic way of exploring what he calls the six core psychological needs** that each of us constantly works to gratify on a predominantly unconscious level.

It is important for us to comprehend the various impetuses behind our everyday choices and behaviors. This will help us to develop an understanding of why we act in certain ways, including some of the unsupportive things that affect us physically, mentally, emotionally, socially and spiritually. We can then think about alternative ways to fulfil our needs in more positive ways, which would go a long way to generate a sense of fulfilment in our lives.

Tony Robbins says that the following six human needs drive our strongest motivations and decide how we prioritize our choices and courses of action in our lives. These needs go gradually upwards, from the predominantly individuality and material stages towards connectivity, dealings and influence in the world. Each person goes through different phases of life at different times, which in turn determine our focal point and needs, with each need playing a pivotal role in creating a fulfilling life in various ways.

The **first four needs** can be classified as "**personality needs,**" for they focus on our individual pursuit for self-fulfilment and accomplishment from a worldly standpoint. The **last two needs** are referred to as **"Needs of the Spirit,"** as they hold the key to finding our deeper sense of true happiness and realization in life – in both the physical and non-physical spheres.

Let's now examine each of these needs:

- **Certainty**

This can be defined as the need for safety, comfort, and consistency, among others. At a very core level, we all crave a basic sense of solidity in the world.

For starters, fulfilling this need gives the assurance of continuing our family lineage. This need also includes working in our chosen occupation and carrying out our daily responsibilities to obtain food, shelter and clothing, as well as nurturing our relationships and securing our endeavors.

However, since the world at large and the lives of those around us, in particular, are constantly evolving, our requirement for certainty sometimes makes us build walls around us, as well as maintain the status quo and even resist change, even when it's beneficial.

- **Variety**

This refers to the requirements for ambiguity, diversity, change and challenge. While all of us long for a sense of security and safety in our lives, we sometimes should also part ways from the known and predictable path with the purpose of allowing ourselves to develop as individuals and find our true path.

The desires for unpredictability and variety break through certainty and stagnation in our lives and facilitate our growth and evolvement. Through this, we break the shackles of past experience and see new possibilities and explore new horizons.

The need to experience variety can, at times, be taken to almost unhealthy levels, especially when our most important impetus is continuous change, for instance, in our job or relationships. While variety is sometimes precisely what we require, in due course of time, **constantly gratifying the need for variety through merely changing our external environment can be detrimental** to experiencing life — and prevent us from experiencing the present moment.

On the optimistic side, variety gives us an objective approach that facilitates our growth both internally and externally and brings change when it is needed, starting with us. **As we generate an authentic shift internally, our external environment will change correspondingly**, without our needing to force the issue and artificially change it, so this does not entail, say, moving to another location or changing our current job.

The above first two needs, certainty and variety, seem to diverge from each other. But these apparently opposing forces work together to make a complete sum total. When we are out of balance with one of these needs, it is often the other that works in the opposite direction to give us a sense of balance.

For instance, let us say that the need for certainty has been over-fulfilled to such an extent that it has led to monotony and dullness. By moving out of our comfort zone and trying something new, we can balance the scales in our life.

- **Significance**

The third human need as we step up progressively on the ladder of human needs is to be recognized **both for who we are as persons and what we do**. This need deals with the necessity for depth, validation, being sought after, and honored. It is imperative that we recognize that we do not exist in silos but as part of a larger whole. To be an effective part of that sum total, we should know that we are playing our part, and in what capacity, as well as be acknowledged for our contribution.

Fulfilling the need for significance is an essential part of **creating our sense of individuality** in the world. The key is not to let ourselves become totally dependent on validation and approval from the outside world, so we can feel at peace with ourselves. If we let this overwhelm us, we might allow it to take over our lives to such an extent that it makes us lose the vision of our own internal compass and voice and limits the intensity of our relationships in various aspects of our lives. It also gives the remote control to our state of mind in other people's hands.

If they feel good about us, we feel good. If they feel bad about us, we feel bad. **It is important to value the opinions and ideas of others, while at the same time not letting them completely cloud and eventually take over our mind**. When we become overly obsessed with the opinions of others and slaves to others' impressions, we risk losing our individuality and uniqueness.

At the same time, it is necessary to be recognized and rewarded, both monetarily and non-monetarily, for our professional contributions, so we can remain motivated. However, we should not be so bound by the expectation of a reward that we stop doing welfare work for society just because we did not get the reward we expected. In such cases, the satisfaction of doing well for others can often be a reward in itself.

- **Love and Connection**

This is the need for relationships, connection and intimacy with others. Human beings have a need to both love and be loved by others and to have a sense of belonging. We crave genuine love and meaningful connections with fellow living beings. The give and take of real warmth and affection is what makes life meaningful.

There are various ways to feel and express our love and feelings for others. This is best done by taking the time and effort to make authentic connections with people, from the heart, by establishing a deep connection with our true self. This naturally aligns with our true inner self and spreads out to establish genuine love and warmth towards others.

The above four needs are commonly referred to as **personality needs**, as they focus on our personal pursuit for self-fulfilment and achievement from a worldly perspective. We shall now examine the remaining two needs, which are the "needs of the spirit," as they are the pathway to a deeper sense of true happiness and fulfilment, both in physical and non-physical terms.

- **Growth**

This encompasses our need for growth at all levels, including **physical, emotional, mental and spiritual**. To both stay alive and flourish, we must grow continuously. Living beings, relationships, and creative endeavours that stop evolving ultimately decline and perish. The need for growth not only relies on, but also nourishes, the first four human needs above, and invigorates our very existence at all levels of our being.

We should be careful, however, not to allow the need for growth to be taken to unrealistic extremes. Sometimes, growth can be so satisfying that our need to fulfil this need prevents us from being fully present in the moment or causes us to defer applying our growth and knowledge in the world, as we are scared of it being not ripe or adequate.

Fulfilling this need is an acknowledgement that growth is a journey and not a destination in itself. For constant growth, it is important to be authentic, allow ourselves to be imperfect and learn, and find genuine ways to share our realizations and discoveries with others.

- **Contribution**

This refers to the need to serve, give to, and think about others, and aim for the benefit of all. Here, we march towards the final step on the ladder by fulfilling our purpose and bringing true value to others' lives. Once we fulfil the above five needs, we automatically progress to the need for contribution, which is giving a genuine sense of value in the true sense of the word.

Contribution arises from a basic desire to give meaning to our lives by making a difference to the world and to leave a legacy that continues to benefit others even after we are gone from this mortal world. There are various ways to fulfil this need, such as to launch a foundation or volunteer to support a cause we believe in or to simply help someone, bring a smile to someone's face, or help someone to find a *bona fide* spiritual path.

The major challenge with the need for contribution is that we can quite rapidly become weighed down with all the causes, people and animals that need help in this world. We can also neglect our domestic responsibilities towards our near and dear ones as we embark on our quest to give back to society.

We can also observe that many people who consider the need for contribution to be paramount over the other five needs sometimes do so at the cost of their own selves and, therefore, do not take proper care of themselves. One of the best ways to express this need is to understand that this need comes not only from our contribution but our very sense of being, by being present in the moment. When we are thus empowered to be, the activities that we engage in are aligned with our core selves and bear great influence.

Depending upon our current situation, such as what stage of life and personal growth we're at, we unsurprisingly value different needs for different reasons. To summarize, we can create a fulfilling and successful life by striking the optimum balance between the six human needs.

CHAPTER 4: KEY TAKEAWAYS

Human behavior is primarily governed by an individual's physiological and psychological needs. Human desires or needs drive individuals to act and behave differently at various stages of life to become happier.

I. Maslow's Hierarchy of Needs

Abraham Maslow, an American psychologist, developed a need theory where he explained how there is a hierarchy to human needs, starting with basic physical needs and ascending to higher intellectual needs. Here is the hierarchy of the six human needs that become the key motivator for happiness at different stages of one's life:

- **Physiological Needs**: related to the survival of the human body, food, shelter, clothing, i.e. basic life necessities
- **Safety Needs**: safety from war, natural disaster, economic safety, health-related safety, etc.
- **Love & Belonging**: need for family, friends, and intimate relationship with someone
- **Esteem**: concern with getting recognition, status, importance, and respect from others

- **Self-Actualization**: the desire to accomplish everything that one can, to become the most one can be
- **Self-Transcendence**: craving for contribution to the world that transcends beyond yourself

II. Inherent Psychological Needs:

Under the Self-Determination Theory, the last level of happiness requires intrinsic motivation, and it is characterized by three innate psychological needs that give us lasting happiness. They are:

- The need for **Human Connection**
- The need for **Mastery**: to be efficacious in whatever once chooses as a career
- The need for **Autonomy**: to not be controlled by anyone and to be able to make decisions independently

III. The Six Core Needs for Fulfillment

Tony Robbins has categorized the human needs to attain fulfillment in two different baskets (1) the four needs of our personality; and (2) the two needs of our spirit, as described below:

- **Certainty**: the need for safety, comfort and consistency

- **Uncertainty**: the need for variety or novelty in life.
- **Significance**: the need to be acknowledged and recognized for what you do
- **Love and Belonging**: the need to both love and be loved by others and to have a sense of belonging
- **Growth**: growth at all levels, including **physical, emotional, mental and spiritual**
- **Contribution**: desire to give meaning to our lives by making a difference to the world

Chapter 5: Neuroscience: Hacking into Happiness D.O.S.E. Daily

****

"Happiness is a choice and a skill, and you can dedicate yourself to learning that skill and making that choice."

~ Naval Ravikant

Over the years, several studies have been conducted on the neuroscience of happiness. Neuroscientists, psychologists and scientists have been studying the correlation of neuroscience with well-being and happiness.

Especially during the last thirty years or so, scientists have gained a much newer, as well as more precise, view of human nature and behavioral changes, primarily through the assimilation of **psychology, which deals with the analysis of the human mind and human behavior**, and **neuroscience, which is concerned with the examination of the physiology of the brain**.

New technologies, developed within the last two decades, have revealed previously undetected neural connections in the human brain. These consist of imaging technologies, for instance, functional magnetic resonance imaging (fMRI) and positron emission tomography (PET), in conjunction with brainwave analysis technologies such as quantitative electroencephalography (QEEG) (also known as brain mapping).

Sophisticated computer analysis of these connections has helped researchers develop an increasing volume of academic work that links the bodily organ, or the brain, with the mind or the human consciousness, which consists of perception, thinking, feeling, and acting.

Analysis of various PET and fMRI studies has shown that there are certain areas of the brain that are more likely to be connected with particular emotions. For the purpose of this book, we shall elaborate on the following two key emotions, namely happiness and sadness.

- **When we experience happiness,** there is increased activity in quite a few areas of the brain, including the right frontal cortex, the precuneus, the left amygdala, and the left insula. During happiness, there are links between awareness, which is represented by the frontal cortex and insula, as well as the feeling center of the brain, or amygdala.

- **When we experience sadness,** there is more activity in the following areas of the brain, namely the right occipital lobe, the left insula, the left thalamus, the amygdala, and the hippocampus. The hippocampus is linked closely with memory, and it can be logically conferred that awareness of certain memories is associated with feeling sad or depressed.

How does happiness look inside the brain?

I found one GIF file that claims to show how happiness looks like inside the brain. Below is the image of what *happiness really looks like:*

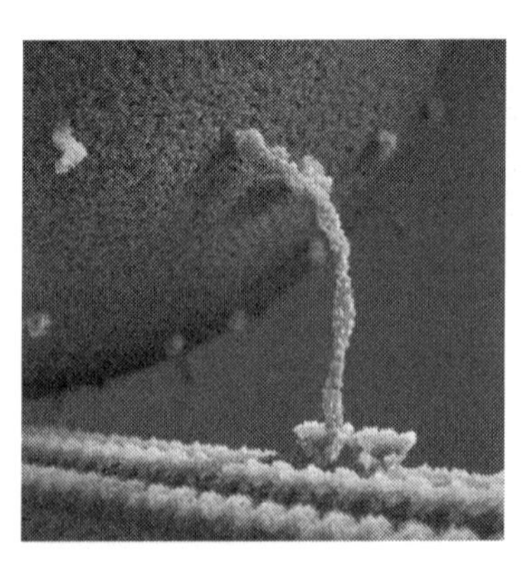

(It shows the molecules of the protein myosin drag a ball of endorphins along an active filament into the inner part of the brain's

parietal cortex, which produces feelings of happiness.)

Since e-book applications don't support showing GIFs, I've put the above image. If you want to see the GIF file showing this cool movement, you can watch this link showing how happiness looks inside the brain[12].

How to Hack into Happiness D.O.S.E.?

The human brain is a complex chemical-generation factory. Whatever emotions we feel throughout the day, be they anger, sadness, love, joy, grief, release multiple chemicals from our brain.

Let's talk about happiness chemicals in our brains.

When we experience happiness, there are four neurochemicals that come into play behind the scenes, namely:

- **D**opamine
- **O**xytocin
- **S**erotonin
- **E**ndorphins

[12] http://www.forastateofhappiness.com/what-happiness-looks-like-in-our-brain/

They can be better remembered as DOSE. They are the neurotransmitters for happiness, or you can call them a happiness dose.

Different events happening in our lives can trigger these neurotransmitters. But instead of simply being a passive spectator and letting life's varied situations influence your feelings, you can choose to be in the driver's seat and incorporate ways that intentionally trigger these neurotransmitters to generate happiness in your life. Each of these four neurotransmitters plays a different kind of role in generating happiness.

Let's examine these chemicals to know what they do and how you can tap into them more often to bring more joy in your life.

Dopamine - Triggers Anticipation

Dopamine is generally considered a happiness drug, but that's a misconception. Scientists originally thought that this substance was related to real pleasure, the pleasure that we've experienced. However, it's recently been argued that dopamine is **more related to anticipatory pleasure and motivation**. In other words, dopamine is actually more involved with creating anticipation than the actual feeling of happiness. It's an emotion for striving.

The notification beeps on your smartphone, ringing of the doorbell and receipt of a mail by post release dopamine as you start to anticipate something new. Dopamine is a molecule that our body produces naturally, and it's the substance that's behind our dreams and biggest secrets. Dopamine **inspires us to take action toward our goals** and also provides us with a rush of reinforcing pleasure once we achieve them. Low levels of dopamine lead to procrastination, self-doubt, and lack of enthusiasm.

It is important to split big goals into smaller goals. In addition to celebrating the major goals, it's imperative that we celebrate sub-goals to enable frequent dopamine release. For instance, go watch a movie while you commemorate a sub-goal.

To ensure a steady pattern for experiencing dopamine, it is also important **to set fresh goals before achieving the current objectives.** To boost an employee's future motivation and productivity, it is also imperative for a leader to recognize the achievements of the team members. These include non-monetary incentives, such as 'thank you emails,' as well as monetary ones, such as performance-based incentives.

Some activities are considered to increase the levels of dopamine in your brain[13]. They are:

- Listening to music
- Dancing
- Getting a message
- Exercising regularly
- Meditating

Oxytocin: Triggers a Feeling of Human Connectedness

The release of oxytocin generates feelings of closeness and trust and makes relationships grow. A study showed that men in monogamous relationships who were given a dose of oxytocin kept lesser physical proximity with other women compared with men who were not administered oxytocin.

It is released by mothers during childbirth and breastfeeding. The blocking of oxytocin even leads animals to reject their offspring. Oxytocin also increases loyalty and is the bonding factor for healthy relationships. It is also known "the cuddle hormone," and among the easiest ways to keep oxytocin flowing is to hug someone. Physical touch not only raises oxytocin but reduces cardiovascular stress and improves the immune system.

---

[13] https://blog.cognifit.com/functions-of-dopamine-serve-you/

This reminds me about one character in a super-hit Hindi movie titled "Munnabhai MBBS", where the protagonist takes admissions at a medical college. He finds that patients with some chronic diseases were treated like 'subjects' of treatment only and no more like humans having emotions. So, he started to give "Jaadu ki Jhappi" (a Hindi word, which means 'a magical hug') to every patient he would meet, and the patients started to feel life and recover faster.

Also, when we give someone a gift, it will also boost their oxytocin levels. You can strengthen your relationship with colleagues and friends by giving gifts to them. So, go shake hands with people, give them a warm hug, and you'll increase the level of oxytocin in yourself and the other person. Paul Zak, an American academician, recommends eight hugs every day.

Want a daily dose of Oxytocin?

Start hugging your spouse, friend or life partner more often, giggle and be more playful with kids, and shake hands more often with friends and colleagues.

Serotonin: Leads to a Feeling of Significance

Serotonin regulates our mood. It flows when we feel important and valuable and is related to being respected in the social hierarchy. Remember, when we were young, we used to run to our mothers to show them any minor achievements, even a small piece of drawing or coloring or solving a small puzzle. But as you grow up, it's not practical or advisable to go to your colleagues or superiors to show them everything small thing that you achieve.

We have fewer avenues available now to show our significance to the world, so most people lack a feeling of significance.

Serotonin is released when we feel significant or important. On the other hand, the lack of serotonin causes loneliness and depression. This is also one of the reasons that people engage in detrimental and attention-seeking activities. These include gangs and criminal activity, which these individuals seek out for the culture and feeling of community that they facilitate and the serotonin they release; these activities are a cry for help.

Barry Jacobs, a Professor of psychology at the Princeton Neuroscience Institute, who has examined the brain mechanisms of sleep, the brain chemical serotonin, and the effects of hallucinogens and other psychoactive drugs on the brain for decades, explains that **most**

antidepressants focus on the production of serotonin.

Remembering past achievements helps our brain to re-live memorable incidents. Serotonin is produced in both real-life cases and when our mind remembers past accomplishments. This is because the brain cannot distinguish between real experiences and imagination. Here, gratitude becomes especially critical, particularly during trying times, for it helps us to visualize all the past positive occurrences in our life.

Exposure to the sun is another very effective means to enhance our serotonin levels, as the skin absorbs ultra-violet rays, which enhance the production of serotonin, as well as Vitamin D. It is important to remember that the ideal time for sun exposure is about 20 minutes a day because too much ultraviolet light can be harmful to our health.

Endorphins: Help Us to Overcome Pain

The word Endorphin is actually composed of two words put together: **Endo** + **Morphine**. **Endo** means internal, i.e. the chemical internally released in our brains. **Morphine** is a chemical that helps one to fight pain. Thus, an endorphin is a chemical internally released in our brain that helps us to fight pain. It's all about masking your pain. The release of endorphins gives an energizing feeling, much like how one feels after an adrenaline rush.

Endorphins assist us in emergency situations; our body releases endorphins in situations where it feels that greater performance is required. For example, when one lifts extra weight in the gym, the brain releases endorphins, which allow the muscles to deliver a better performance. Endorphins are released to soothe us when we experience pain and stress and assist in lessening uneasiness. The "runners high" experienced while running is a consequence of the release of endorphins. It acts like morphine, as an analgesic and sedative, and reduces the perception of pain.

Exercise and laughter are the simplest methods to facilitate endorphin release. This includes even the expectation of laugher, such as watching a funny movie. **Dark chocolate and certain scented oils** can also enhance serotonin levels.

According to one study, researchers concluded that it is imperative to judge **not only the amount of emotion experienced, but the duration of positive emotions experienced**. The time period of activity in particular brain circuits, even for comparatively lesser amounts of time, can predict the presence of a person's positive emotions minutes, or even a few hours, later.

The neural pattern observed by the researchers, particularly in the **ventral striatum**, foretold enhanced levels of well-being in other studies too. They also said that kindness and empathy towards others might help increase one's ability to take pleasure in, as well as cultivate positive emotions.

If you really implement the principles of neuroscience for happiness, you can almost instantly generate happiness by doing the activities that trigger the release of happiness D.O.S.E. It is like having access to the happiness switch that you just need to press and immediately experience happiness. You just need the willingness to press the switch, and your happiness can arrive in no time.

CHAPTER 5: KEY TAKEAWAYS

Our brain is one of the most complex and sophisticated chemical factories on the planet. Behind all our emotions, be they happiness, sadness, love, greed, anger, there is an interplay between multiple chemicals happening inside our brains.

To consistently experience feelings of happiness, we need to find out the ways and ensure that we trigger the release of four primary chemicals in our brain. Commonly stated as an acronym, DOSE, these four chemicals, when released, make us happier.

- **D**opamine: triggered by anticipation and inspires us to take action towards goals.
- **O**xytocin: a feeling of human connectedness; you can release more by hugging your loved ones or shaking hands.
- **S**erotonin: leads to feeling significant; try to recall past achievements to release this.
- **E**ndorphins: helps us to fight pain; exercise, on a regular basis, releases more endorphins.

In a nutshell, for a daily D.O.S.E. of happiness, engage in the following activities:

- Exercise (e.g. run, walk)
- Laugh/cry

- Hug and/or shake hands with your friends
- Anticipate something good. Book your mini-vacation, maybe just a small weekend. When you are anticipating something, you are happier.
- Set and achieve goals
- Build social connections. Appreciate others for their good work. Accept accountability for certain activities, and enjoy being acknowledged.

Chapter 6: Habits for Personal Happiness

****

"What we think or what we know or what we believe is, in the end, of little consequence. The only consequence is what we do."

~ John Ruskin

Our state of mind from moment to moment depends on what kind of thoughts and emotions we are *allowing* consciously or unconsciously to wander in our heads. One way is to let them wildly run and unconsciously generate whatever emotions they produce. The other way is to consciously observe them and take control of them to direct them in the way that you want.

Though it's not entirely possible to stop your thoughts, you can very well change the direction of your thoughts. Let's understand this with some facts and experiments. Every day, your mind generates around 60,000 thoughts, as various internet articles suggest.

That's like 2500 thoughts every hour and approximately 40 thoughts every minute. That's a huge number, isn't it?

However, 95% of those thoughts are repetitive.

Can you regularly survive seven days a week and thirty days a month by eating the same kind of food?

Obviously, your answer will be a BIG NO. Why?

Because you will feel the need for uncertainty (in the form of novelty). Moreover, food is tangible; you can see it with your eyes and, thus, make decisions more objectively.

You are so careful, when feeding your body, to have a variety of options, but why this is not so in the case of your mind? Why do you consistently allow your mind to be consumed by the same kind of thoughts?

Here are few reasons.

First, they are intangible; you can just imagine and feel them, and secondly, they occur too rapidly and consistently. And lastly, but most importantly, you are too closely engaged or involved in your thoughts.

When you get so close to something, you can't see it clearly. You know it already by experience, but let's try to experience it again. Take any small object; it could be your smartphone or TV, your remote, or maybe an apple or anything that is big enough to cover your eye. Now bring it closer to your eyes; make it so close to your eyes so that it's almost touching your eyelashes.

Now try to realize this for yourself. Though you intellectually, and by experience, know what that object is, honestly ask yourself if your eyes can tell what the object is when it is brought so much closer to your eyes. Maybe, to bring more objectivity to this experience (so you are not influenced by your prior experience with the object), close your eyes first and ask someone to bring an object to close to your eyes, and then open your eyes. Can you tell what the object is?

If you did this experiment correctly, you'd just make a wild guess but not a certain answer. This is because our eyes need some distance to focus on and create an imagery of the object we are looking at. Without maintaining some distance, you can't really see or analyze anything. The same applies to your thoughts. When you start seeing your thoughts and emotions from a distance, you direct them differently.

Now, let's do another simple experiment that will help you **start seeing the separate identity of your thoughts/emotions and, thus, help you disengage with them.** Take a pen and paper or start typing in your phone/laptop, or wherever you can write something, and look at it through your eyes.

Step 1: Write down the list of your **physical belongings**; examples could be your house, car, clothes, etc. List a few of them for a better experience.

Step 2: Now make a **list of people** who you refer to as 'my', could be 'my father', mother, teacher, best friend, spouse, child, etc. Again, write down many of them for a better experience.

Step 3: You covered outside things and outside people in the first two steps. Let's come a little bit closer, and now, write down about how you talk about **your body**, like 'my' hand, foot, face, etc.

This experiment may seem quite absurd to you, as you know all these things already, but bear with me for a moment. Sometimes big realizations take place as a result of observing simple things. So, let's continue.

In Step 1 to Step 3, you could see everything that was tangible and visible through your own eyes. While objects in Step 1 and 2 were not part of your body, Step 3 was closer, as you observed your own body as your possession (and not YOU).

Step 4: Now, in Step 4, you will look at invisible things: **your thoughts and emotions.** You can't see them, but you can experience them running inside of you consistently. Think, how do you mention them? Again, you'd use the prefix 'my'? You would say my thoughts, my emotions, my feelings, etc.

Now try to understand the difference in all the four steps. What was happening here?

The more things started coming closer to you, the more you consider them as a part of you. And when they come so closer like your thoughts or emotions, you even start to think them as YOU only.

With such proximity, such thoughts and emotions start taking the form of your identity, and that becomes the root cause of living a life like a victim instead of being in the driver's seat. When you think of yourself as a particular thought or emotion, you can't not behave other than that. If you think yourself as someone who is shy or not good enough, etc., what kinds of actions will generate from such an identity? You know it very well.

Only when you can see your thoughts clearly as some separate thing can you can start taking control of their direction. Why am I putting so much emphasis on disengaging with your thoughts and emotions here? Because we are talking about building a happier brain, and **to experience happiness in every situation requires a deeper sense of awareness.**

Self-awareness means an awareness about oneself. It's not just being aware of your body parts or internal organs; it's more about being aware of your thoughts and emotions. Once you are aware of the quality of any thought or emotions, only then you can use your consciousness to alter the direction of your thoughts.

Your level of happiness will significantly grow as you increase your level of self-awareness.

The habits we will discuss will do the work of enhancing your level of self-awareness i.e. they will make it working on autopilot basis, so you get the benefits without every time pushing yourself hard.

Let's now talk about some key habits that will enhance your personal habits:

- **Daily Gratitude Practice**

First things first.

Gratitude is arguably the most important thing to do if you want to achieve a happy state of mind. The key is to start your day right. When you wake up, THANK GOD for everything you've been blessed with.

Count at least three things you are grateful for. The first and foremost you should be grateful for is that you woke up this morning again.

Congratulate yourself and feel gratitude that you are again alive. You and I take this life for granted, but did you know a huge number of people did not wake up today? Did you know that 55.3 million people die each year? This means that 6,316 people are dying every hour or two people every second[14]. And you and I are not among them.

Now look at your loved ones, your family or friends; they, too, are alive. You didn't get any shocking calls in the middle of the night from any of your loved ones, which means that your family and close friends are all well. You can never take this precious life for granted when every two seconds, one person is dying. So, start feeling grateful for that.

If you are reading this book on an electronic device or can buy it using your computer and internet connection, you are way better off than most of the population on the planet; this is something else to feel grateful for.

Remember your wealth/income assessment test that you probably did in one of the previous chapters at www.globalrichlist.com? If you did not take the test, please do it now. Trust me; you have many more reasons to be grateful than you think.

---

[14] http://www.ecology.com/birth-death-rates/

However, let's be clear, at no stage does feeling grateful mean that one should become complacent and lazy. No, we should always give our best, yet accept that things will not always work out the way we want while always being grateful at every level, be it material, physical, emotional, mental and spiritual.

In one experiment, Martin Seligman, founder of the positive psychology movement, studied 47 severely depressed individuals. This study involved two unusual components. First, participants focused their attention on things that were proven to increase happiness – specifically, an exercise called the three blessings, in which people wrote down three things that had gone well that day – instead of the source or nature of their unhappiness, which is where many mental health interventions focus. Second, communities were allowed to form, which encouraged people to pay attention to the happiness-inducing exercises.

Depression in 94 percent of the participants dropped significantly, from clinically severe to clinically mild-to-moderate symptoms. **The impact was similar to the effects of medication and cognitive therapy combined**. Perhaps any behavior change brought about by leaders, managers, therapists, trainers, or coaches is primarily a function of their ability to induce others to focus their attention on specific ideas, closely enough, often enough, and for a long enough time.

Sonja Lyubomirsky, a psychology professor at the University of California and a happiness researcher, states:

"People who are **consistently grateful** have been found to be relatively **happier**, more **energetic**, more **hopeful,** and report experiencing more frequent positive emotions. They also tend to be more **helpful and empathic**, more spiritual and religious, more **forgiving**, and less materialistic than others who are less predisposed to gratefulness. Furthermore, the more a person is inclined to gratitude, the less likely he or she is to be depressed, anxious, lonely, envious, or neurotic."

She talks about a research study demonstrating the fact that people who kept **a weekly gratitude journal for ten weeks** in which they noted five things for which they were thankful were significantly happier than those who didn't.

Happiness happens as soon as you practice gratitude. When you are expressing gratitude, you can never be sad at the same time; try it out for yourself. Psychological research has found that people who practice gratitude consistently report a host of benefits[15]:

Physical

- Stronger immune systems
- Less bothered by aches and pains
- Lower blood pressure
- Exercise more and take better care of their health
- Sleep longer and feel more refreshed upon waking

Psychological

- Higher levels of positive emotions
- More alert, alive, and awake
- More joy and pleasure
- More optimism and happiness

Social

- More helpful, generous, and compassionate
- More forgiving
- More outgoing
- Feel less lonely and isolated

How to make gratitude a part of everyday life?

Simple. It doesn't take more than two minutes. As you wake up in the morning, try to count

---

15 http://greatergood.berkeley.edu/article/item/why_gratitude_is_good

three good things in our life. They don't need to be massive things; they can be even smaller things like good sleep, the comfy feeling of your bed, a cool breeze outside your window, or seeing your partner or kids sleeping and relaxed. These simple things could be reasons for feeling grateful or anything else which you feel good about.

Some people use a gratitude journal, where they write every day a few things they are most grateful for. You can write in it anywhere, in any simple notebook. Whether you think about it or write about it, the key is to be consistent about it.

- Write three to five things about which you are grateful every morning.
- During the day, look at the things that are going well in your life and feel grateful for them. It reinforces this habit.
- Do the same thing before going to sleep.

When you hit a rough patch, as everyone invariably does, this practice is an absolute lifesaver, in every sense of the word.

"If you aren't grateful for what you already have, what makes you think you would be

happy with more?" ~Roy T. Bennett

Practice it, and you will start to attract abundance and joy in your life. The key is to say thank you from the heart, sincerely and with feeling.

- **Breathe Deeply**

Sometimes the main cause of stress is that we don't do that basic thing which is most necessary for survival, which is breathing properly.

In fact, every thought and every emotion causes a corresponding reaction in the breath. For example, when you're angry, you breathe faster; when you're sad, your exhalation is longer than your inhalation. And when you're happy, you breathe normally and peacefully. Next time, whenever you are in these different moods, just assess the pace of breath and see for yourself.

What does all this tell us? It simply means that you can change how you feel simply by changing the pattern of your breathing. Studies show that breathing practices can **reduce nervousness, sleeplessness, post-traumatic stress disorder, and depression**, to name just a few. Modern science has just begun to comprehend the role of breath control, or pranayama, to enhance focus and improve energy levels; it has been practiced for thousands of years by yogis.

Notice the next time you feel stressed. Just close your eyes (obviously when you're not driving or in the middle of an important meeting) and take a few deep breaths. You'll feel better immediately. Do this regularly; in fact, as often as possible. Try it for yourself, and you will see the results.

Also, following these simple active breathing practices for a few minutes can get you in an instant state of calm and peacefulness.

Alternate Nostril Breathing

It's known as Anulom Vilom pranayama, one of the most effective yoga practices. Alternate nostril breathing is said to calm the mind in just a few minutes. It is an excellent practice to do before meditating or to calm intense emotions. It is safe to do anytime, for as long as you like.

Here is how you can start doing it **just for five minutes a day**:

1. Sit comfortably, with your spine straight, and close your eyes.

2. Use your right thumb and little finger to alternately block one nostril so you can only breathe through the other nostril. Start by exhaling out the left nostril; then, breathe in through the same nostril.

3. Switch sides after each inhalation. Breathe normally at your own relaxed pace, giving some attention to completing the exhalation, without forcing it.

If you make this a daily practice in your life, you will start to see your thoughts and emotions clearly, because you've already learned how to watch the sensations in your body by just observing the breath. This way, you will not get entangled in a compulsive, repetitive thinking cycle; rather, it will instil a sense of relaxation in your brain, and you will invite solutions to your problems.

- **Empty Your Head by Journaling Daily**

You learned already how heavy our mind's workload is; we deal with thousands of thoughts running through our heads every hour.

In our journey to build a happier brain, we have to generate happier thoughts consciously. But our minds are still in primitive age and inclined to think negative thoughts more than positive ones. Of course, the primitive age required us to think negatively in every situation because ignoring a little noise in the bushes could have meant becoming prey to some wild animal. Though we have physically evolved, the reptilian brain that's responsible for our survival generates negative thinking.

So, what do we do about it? The solution is to create another brain out of our brain: a **brain that does the 'storage' work on paper**, where you can dump out whatever is going on in your head and make your head empty once again. This process is called journaling. Having a separate paper brain outside will empty your head and make room for you to control your thinking process by directing your thoughts in the way that you want.

In fact, journaling is considered amongst the most beneficial kind of writing. One 2005 study[16] found that the kind of "expressive writing" often connected with journaling is especially therapeutic. The study found that participants who wrote about traumatic, stressful, or emotional events were significantly less likely to get sick and were ultimately less seriously affected by trauma than their non-journaling counterparts.

You can distance yourself from your thoughts and emotions if you consistently start seeing them on paper. Precisely, your conscious

---

[16] http://apt.rcpsych.org/content/11/5/338.full

memory and RAM (just like a computer memory) should not be used for storing the running thoughts; rather, it should be used for creating new ideas.

Writing empties the conscious space, so that much better work can be undertaken by the mind, such as generating fresh ideas and thoughts. Moreover, you can now see what's going on more objectively. You can distinguish if something is just a fearful, negative thought or if it is really worth paying attention to.

Journaling also makes you more grateful and happier because you can see all the good things happening in your life now.

What should you write in your journal?

Hal Elrod, in his book *The Miracle Morning*, talks about six morning rituals that one should follow to kickstart the day with full energy and to optimize one's potential. He coins the acronym S.A.V.E.R.S., which stands for Silence, Affirmation, Visualization, Exercise, Reading, and Scribble. The last one, scribbling, means journaling as part of your morning routine.

He also specifically suggests what one should cover in one's journal, as follows:

- What are you grateful for regarding your previous day?

- What are your specific accomplishments?
- What are your specific desired areas of improvement?
- What are the top five things that you must do today to take your life to the next level?

Sonja Lyubomirsky, in her book *The How of Happiness*, recommends using the **Best Possible Selves Diary Method** as a journaling technique to bring in happiness.

Here is how it works:

Sit in a quiet place, and take twenty to thirty minutes to think about what you expect your life to be one, five, or ten years from now.

Visualize a future for yourself in which everything has turned out the way that you've wanted. You have tried your best, worked hard, and achieved all your goals. Now write down what you imagine. This writing exercise, in a sense, **puts your optimistic 'muscles' into practice**. Even if thinking about the brightest future for yourself doesn't come naturally at first, it may get there with time and training. Amazing things can come about as a result of writing.

Also, Neil Pasricha, another happiness researcher, recommends a **20 minutes replay exercise**. He says writing for 20 minutes about a positive experience is a GREAT way to boost your happiness. Scientists call it savoring.

I've told you many approaches to journaling, as I didn't want you to just limit on what has worked for me only. Everyone is different, so you may prefer a different technique to express your thoughts and emotions. The whole objective of doing this journaling exercise is to empty your head and help you see your thoughts and emotions from a distance.

If you still want to know more about the ways of journaling, you will also find this link from Robin Sharma: https://www.robinsharma.com/article/how-to-keep-a-journal to get a detailed perspective of journal-writing and what it should contain.

Again, ten minutes of daily journaling will start to enhance the level of your clarity and bring a smile to your face. Since you can see very clearly on paper and identify what matters and what's worth ignoring, you become more focused and action-oriented.

- **Regular Exercise**

As you already know, endorphins cause happiness by masking pain. Physical exercise is one of the best ways to release endorphins and other helpful chemicals from our brain. Also, studies show that it releases BDNF (Brain-Derived Neurotrophic Factors) that works as a

RESET switch, which means that it helps you get out of routine thinking and generate new ideas. You become more creative and solution-oriented. Exercise helps you lower the levels of cortisol, the stress hormone, so you can easily overcome any stressful situations.

An impressive study of physical activity was published in the Archives of Internal Medicine in 1999. The researchers recruited men and women fifty years old and over, all of them suffering from **clinical depression**, and divided them randomly into three groups.

The first group was assigned to four months of aerobic exercise, the second group to four months of antidepressant medication (Zoloft), and the third group to both. The assigned exercise involved three supervised forty-five-minute sessions per week of cycling or walking/jogging at moderate to high intensity.

Remarkably, by the end of the four-month intervention period, all three groups had experienced relief from their depression and reported fewer dysfunctional attitudes and **increased happiness** and **self-esteem**. **Aerobic exercise was just as effective at treating depression as Zoloft,** or as a combination of exercise and Zoloft. Yet exercise is a lot less expensive, usually with no side effects, apart from soreness.

Perhaps even more remarkably, six months later, participants who had "remitted" (recovered) from their depressions were less likely to relapse if they had been in the exercise group (six months ago!) than if they had been in the medication group.

John Ratey, in his book *Spark: The Revolutionary New Science of Exercise and Brain* states: "A regular exercise regime stimulates the release of positive neurotransmitters, like dopamine (which encourages motivation, attention, and pleasure), serotonin (which enhances learning, mood, and self-esteem), and norepinephrine (which leads to arousal and alertness). The best part: exercise expedites the production of BDNF (brain-derived neurotrophic factor), a protein that Ratey has dubbed "Miracle-Gro for the brain".

The above studies and research already show that exercise has many health and mental benefits. It enhances physical health, including strength, stamina and agility, and improves creative thinking and cognitive skills. It is also an instant mood elevator, as it increases the production of endorphins, the body's anti-depressants.

And there are so many options we can choose from. There are numerous indoor sports such as racquetball, squash, basketball, table-tennis and badminton, and outdoor sports such as tennis, track and field, baseball, and soccer. These are in addition to walking and jogging, working out at the gym, pilates, and yoga, to name just a few.

With so many options at our disposal, and after knowing all the benefits it offers, there is definitely no excuse not to exercise, except laziness and lack of commitment to improve our lives. You can consider just taking two brisk walks every day as a habit, and that will keep you happy. Get started with just 15 minutes a day if you can't do more, but get started.

With the kind of benefits that exercise offers to bring happiness and the amount of time it requires to do, you can easily calculate the return on your time invested doing exercise.

- **Practice Mindfulness**

As I stated at the beginning of this chapter, we need to increase our level of self-awareness in such a way that we can disengage with our thoughts and emotions.

Meditation is the process by which we go about deepening our attention and awareness, refining them, and putting them to greater practical use in our lives. Mindfulness is a form of meditation in which you simply focus on your breath as an anchor. It's derived from an ancient Buddhism technique call Anapansati Yoga. Anapana is awareness of natural breath coming in and going out. With only a few minutes of practice, it can make your mind happy, calm and concentrated.

Let's be clear; you don't need to follow any specific religion to practice mindfulness. Though it originated from Buddhism, it's now more of a neuroscience-proven technique to improve your well-being.

Mindfulness entered into the mainstream of the western world primarily for a therapeutic purpose. In 1979, Jon Kabat-Zinn, an American professor emeritus of the Center for Mindfulness in Medicine, Health Care, and Society at the University of Massachusetts Medical School, sparked the application of mindfulness ideas and practices in medicine. He started a Mindfulness-Based Stress Reduction (MBSR) program for treating the chronically ill people.

Neuroscience has already proved that practising mindfulness can literally change your brain structure. Sara Lazar, a neuroscientist at Harvard Medical School, used the MRI technology to look at very fine and detailed brain structures to observe the inner physical changes in the brain while a person is performing certain tasks, including yoga and meditation.

In one of her studies[17], she engaged people who had never meditated before and put them

---

17 https://www.ncbi.nlm.nih.gov/pmc/articles/PMC3004979/

through a Mindfulness-Based Stress Reduction training program, where they took a weekly class and were told to perform mindfulness exercises, including body scans, mindful yoga, and sitting meditation every day for 30 to 40 minutes. Lazar wanted to test the participants for the positive effects of mindfulness meditation on their psychological well-being and the alleviation of symptoms of various disorders such as anxiety, depression, eating disorder, insomnia, or chronic pain.

After eight weeks, she found out that the brain volume increased in the:

i. Hippocampus: a seahorse-shaped structure responsible for learning, storage of memories, spatial orientation, and the regulation of emotions.
ii. Temporoparietal Junction: the area where temporal and parietal lobes meet, and which is responsible for empathy and compassion.

On the other hand, the one place that brain volume decreased was the amygdala, an almond-shaped structure responsible for triggering the fight-or-flight response as a reaction to a threat, whether real or only perceived.

Kelly McGonigal, psychologist, researcher, and author of the book, *The Willpower Instinct* explains the benefits of meditation:

"Neuroscientists have now found that when we make ourselves sit and instruct our brain to meditate, not only does it get better at meditating, but it develops a wide range of self-control skills, including attention, focus, stress management, impulse control, and self-awareness. Another study found that eight weeks of daily meditation practice led to increased self-awareness in everyday life, as well as increased grey matter in corresponding areas of the brain. Meditation increases blood flow to the prefrontal cortex in much the same way that lifting weights increases blood flow to your muscles. The brain appears to adapt to exercise in the same way that muscles do, getting both bigger and faster in order to get better at what you ask of it."

Tim Ferriss, bestselling author of *The Tools of Titans.*, also hosts a widely popular podcast show called "*The Tim Ferris Show*". He has already interviewed more than two hundred people from diverse backgrounds, including business tycoons, top sports athletes, the best creative minds around the world, like Arnold Schwarzenegger, Jamie Foxx, Edward Norton, Tony Robbins, Maria Sharapova, Peter Thiel, Amanda Palmer, Malcolm Gladwell, and many more. Tim categorically states that one of the most common rituals or daily practices followed by more than 80% of these interviewees is that they have adopted some form of meditation or a mindfulness practice in their daily routine: a consistent pattern of this secluded practice of being with their own self.

Unless someone has been hiding under the cave for a decade or so, the benefits of mindfulness practices are now widely acknowledged and adopted by lots of high performers in their daily routine. I hope that you are already convinced about the benefits of mindfulness. So, let's see how to do this practice and then incorporate it into our daily lives.

Mindfulness meditation expert Sam Harris compares doing meditation like walking on a rope: easy to explain but difficult to master. He then goes on to describe the steps need to do your mindfulness practice, as described below[18].

Meditation Instructions:

- Sit comfortably, with your spine erect, either in a chair or cross-legged on a cushion.

- Close your eyes, take a few deep breaths, and feel the points of contact between your body and the chair or floor. Notice the sensations associated with sitting—feelings of pressure, warmth, tingling, vibration, etc.

[18] https://www.samharris.org/blog/item/how-to-meditate

- Gradually become aware of the process of breathing. Pay attention to wherever you feel your breath most clearly—either at the nostrils or in the rising and falling of your abdomen.

- Allow your attention to rest in the mere sensation of breathing. (There is no need to control your breath. Just let it come and go naturally.)

- Every time your mind wanders, gently return it to the sensation of breathing.

- As you focus on your breath, you will notice that other perceptions and sensations continue to appear: sounds, feelings in the body, emotions, etc. Simply notice these phenomena as they emerge in the field of awareness, and then return to the sensation of breathing.

- The moment that you observe that you have been lost in thought, notice the present thought itself as an object of consciousness. Then return your attention to the breath—or to whatever sounds or sensations arise in the next moment.

- Continue in this way until you can merely witness all objects of consciousness—sights, sounds, sensations, emotions, and even thoughts themselves—as they arise and pass away.

- Don't fall.

Those who are new to the practice generally find it useful to hear instructions of this kind spoken aloud, in the form of guided meditation.

There are plenty of guided meditation apps available these days that can help you to do a guided meditation. You can just Google 'guided meditation apps' to find many good, free apps instantly.

➢ Random Act of Kindness

> ***"The best way to cheer yourself is to try to cheer someone else up."***
>
> ***~ Mark Twain***

Let's understand this with a short story.

An old man walked across the beach until he came across a young boy throwing something into the breaking waves. Upon closer inspection, the old man could see that the boy was tossing stranded starfish from the sandy beach back into the ocean.

"What are you doing, young man?" He asked.

“If the starfish are still on the beach when the sun rises, they will die,” the boy answered.

“That is ridiculous. There are thousands of miles of beach and millions of starfish. It doesn’t matter how many you throw in; you can’t make a difference.”

“It matters to this one,” the boy said as he threw another starfish into the waves. “And it matters to this one.”

You might have already heard the story, and the message is very clear. Just get into any random act of kindness on a daily basis. It gives you instant happiness.

Let me share one such personal example. The other day, I was driving in the morning on a secluded road. I noticed a man walking with heavy bags in his hands. His wife was holding two young kids in her and one more walking along with them. They were waving their hands at vehicles to flag down a lift to the next bus station so that they could ride a bus to their destination.

At first, I drove past them thinking, why should I get involved? I thought that they would find someone else or that maybe they were used to walking so much. But, after continuing to drive a few meters ahead, I thought that I should help them. I took my car back and offered them a lift.

The kind of relief and happiness I could see on their faces gave me an instant blast of happiness and made me feel good about myself.

This quote below from great Albert Einstein shows how our happiness enhances when we serve others. He said: *"From the standpoint of daily life, however, there is one thing we do know:* ***that we are here for the sake of each other*** *— above all, for those upon whose smile and well-being our own happiness depends, and also for the countless unknown souls with whose fate we are connected by a bond of sympathy.*

Many times a day, I realize how much my own outer and inner life is built upon the labors of my fellow men, both living and dead, and ***how earnestly I must exert myself in order to give in return as much as I have received****."*

In your day-to-day life, you could show many random acts of kindness, maybe saying thank you or being kind to your colleagues in your interactions. You can offer a few words of optimism to someone who is stressed and depressed. If you are conscious about it, you'll find many opportunities during your day to build this habit.

Spread kindness around, and it will come back to you with a manifold of happiness.

- **Surround yourself with optimistic and cheerful people:**

We should very carefully choose the company we keep. Our environment defines us, as it is contagious. We should consciously discard those toxic relationships that pull us down instead of uplifting us. And we should cultivate and nurture those relationships that uplift us.

Our association has a direct bearing on our internal growth and our daily mood and general well-being. As Jim Rohn rightly said, *"You are the average of the five people you spend the most time with."* It is imperative to spend quality time with family and friends. We are social beings and need to have a sense of belonging.

A strong support system of family and close friends is necessary to share all the good times. In addition, this very support system is where we can share the most confidential things. They also help us to tide over difficult times, not only in the form of emotional support but also because they can give us a completely new outlook about how to view a particular situation, as well as provide fresh ideas and solutions.

"Good things happen in your life when you surround yourself with positive people."

~ Roy Bennett

Therefore, on a regular basis, choose to spend time with people who elevate you on your journey, and avoid people who have a negative outlook towards life and don't want to change their lives.

CHAPTER 6: KEY TAKEAWAYS

Self-awareness is the key to taking control of your mind. The way to self-awareness is getting disengaged from your thoughts and emotions.

To experience happiness on a consistent basis requires a deeper sense of awareness.

The following habits will help you disengage with your mind as well as build happiness in your personal life:

- Practice **Gratitude**
- **Breathe** deeply
- **Exercise** regularly
- **Empty your head** through journaling
- Practice **Mindfulness**
- **Surround yourself** with quality people
- Do some **random act of kindness** daily

The best part is that you don't need a great deal of time to inculcate these habits in your daily life.

Assuming you are too busy, still if you could just spare just half an hour, you can instil above habits in your daily routine. To be specific, practicing gratitude shouldn't take more than 2 minutes, journaling can be done in 5 minutes, breathing and mindfulness practices can be done in under 15 minutes. You can do intensive exercise for 10 minutes every day, and do a bit more over the weekend.

And this additional half an hour can be generated by sleeping and thus waking up 30 minutes earlier. Maybe you can cut down some time out of other activities that take your time in the morning or in the evening.

Even half hour of regular practice will start to reward you in the form of higher self-awareness, reduced stress, and bring more calm and joy in your life, in a matter of few weeks.

Chapter 7: Habits for Professional Happiness

****

"People rarely succeed unless they are having fun in what they are doing."

~ Dale Carnegie

Work is the most integral part of our lives. We spend 8-12 hours every day working, and then a few more hours thinking about work. Time spent at work can be a source of fulfilment and accomplishment, and for some people, work can be the cause of anxiety, worry and even depression. It depends on how we consider our work in most cases.

Martin Seligman talks about the three kinds of 'work orientation': **a job, a career, and a calling**.

As he points out, **you go to a job strictly for the paycheck**. Punch the clock and get paid.

You have a **career to enjoy the benefits of advancement** and mastery of a given domain.

A **calling** (or vocation), on the other hand, is a **passionate commitment to work** for its own sake.

Any job can become a calling, and any calling can become a job.

A physician who views the work as a Job and is simply interested in making a good income does not have a Calling, while a garbage collector who sees the work as making the world a cleaner, healthier place could have a Calling.

Our work creates our identity about who we are. The majority of people work with other people. I'd say 99% of the population works with close interaction with other people, unlike a few categories of people like writers, painters, etc., whose work doesn't require them to interact much on a regular basis with the outside world.

Let's talk about the majority now. When our work and professional career takes up more than half of our waking life on a daily basis (1/3 of our time goes to sleep and rest), it becomes really important to master the art of happiness while working and also dealing with the outside world.

In this section, we will talk about what habits will help us to generate happiness at our work.

- **Be Punctual**

Reaching work on time, and preferably before time, allows us to collect our thoughts and respond, rather than react, to various situations we might encounter in our daily lives. Whether you are an entrepreneur or an employee, you should always aim to reach your workplace a few minutes before time and start your workday on the right note.

> ***"Lose an hour in the morning, and you will spend all day looking for it."***
>
> ***— Richard Whately***

Also, a job well begun is half the job done. If you start your work early, you take advantage of a great beginning in a less-distracted environment with an intense focus on the activity. It keeps stress at bay because you are proactive, taking the challenges head-on, rather than being dominated by your work.

Arriving on time to the office in the morning or to attend some important meeting gives you a sense of self-confidence and commitment to your work. Being punctual helps you to stay on plan and deliver your best performance.

So be punctual at your workplace, and arrive on time at your meetings and for every other occasion where it's necessary.

➢ Harness the Power of Starting Any Communication Well

In any interaction, what we are first exposed to influences our behavior. Psychologists call this "priming."

Research shows that how we start a conversation predicts how it is likely to turn out. If a conversation starts negatively, it tends to continue negatively. Start it positively, and you've primed it for awesome.

> ***"Every word we say during our day counts, but especially at the beginning of each new interaction."***
>
> ***~ Michelle Gielan***

Michelle Gielan, in her book "Broadcasting Happiness", explains the concept of Power Leads. *"A power lead is a positive, optimistic, and inspiring beginning to a conversation or other communication that sets the tone for the ensuing social script."*

The power lead is one of the most crucial steps to motivate a team, connect more deeply with colleagues, or to set the stage for higher levels of creativity because it helps our brains focus on growth-producing areas. Since **humans are socialized to mimic one another**, the people you are connecting with often reciprocate the positive nature of a power lead as you continue to connect.

There are some examples of power leads in different situations:

Meetings: Start a meeting with five minutes of gratitude or positive stories about the progress you and your team have made.

Parents: When you first see your kids after school (or a sports activity/etc.), start by asking them what the best part of their day was.

Email: Start your email with a simple, *"Hi NAME! Hope you're doing great!"*, then get into whatever you need to discuss.

- **Practice Getting in the State of Flow Regularly**

On a daily basis, you should try to get into a state of flow.

There are few requisites to get into a state of flow:

- Spend at least two to three hours in a distraction-free environment. Generally, it's best to choose the morning and before noon hours, as you are full of energy and willpower to handle challenging tasks. Put your phone on silence mode, and try to avoid distractions as much as your environment supports. Most people can't control the distraction in their work environment, so the better option is to start working early on your important projects before other people start coming to the workplace.

- You need to increase the intensity of your focus on the work at hand and not let anything else get in the way of your work.

- The work you are doing must be a stretch beyond your current abilities so that you feel challenged to do it. Remember, human beings love growth, and challenges give them growth.

As you learned already in the previous sections from Mihaly Csikszentmihalyi, the author of *Flow: The Psychology of Optimal Experience*, the optimal state of human experience is found when we are engaged in activities that stretch us such that the challenges match our skills. Too much challenge leads to anxiety, and too little challenge creates boredom. So, you should find the right match to get into a state of flow. Strive for finding flow daily, and you'll be exposed to happiness more often at your workplace.

- **Unplug Completely**

Work, work and more work will not only lead to chronic fatigue and burnout but will also make us more one-dimensional in our thinking. We miss out on meaningful times that we could have spent with family and friends. It is important to find a hobby or cause that we could get involved in and make the time for it.

Are you allocating time to your RECOVERY as much as your "ON" phases? Remember that it's not that we work too hard, but that we don't recover enough. Jim Loehr, a performance psychologist, in his book called *Toughness Training for Life*, emphasizes this formula:
It's important to understand that only rarely does the volume of stress defeat us; far more often, the agent of defeat is insufficient capacity for recovery after the stress. **Great stress simply requires great recovery**. Your goal in toughness, therefore, is to be able to spike powerful waves of stress followed by equally powerful troughs of recovery. So, here is an essential Toughness Training Principle: Work hard. Recover equally hard.

From a training perspective, then, training recovery should receive as much attention as training stress. Unfortunately, that is rarely the case. He puts it this way: "***Precisely, the***

stress is the stimulus for growth. Recovery is when you grow." Therefore, at times, unplug totally from work; focus on recovering.

Play any sport. Get involved with social causes, such as the education of underprivileged children. This will revitalize you when you get back to work again as well as make your life more meaningful and rewarding at all levels.

- **Be Coachable and Receptive to Feedback and Suggestions**

A 1997 study[19] of 31 public-sector managers by researchers Gerald Olivero, K. Denise Bane, and Richard E. Kopelman found that a training program alone increased productivity by 28 percent, but the addition of follow-up coaching to the training increased productivity 88 percent.

Therefore, instead of becoming defensive, you should take criticism constructively and think of the person who is criticizing us as a well-wisher who wants us to improve and grow. At the same time, we must learn to filter out criticism from people that are designed to demoralize us. On a regular basis, if you change your attitude and become more receptive to feedback about your performance, it's just a matter of time; you'll

[19] https://www.strategy-business.com/article/06207

start to master your work and get into states of flow more often.

➢ Network Extensively

As someone rightly said, "Your network is your net worth." People who create networks around them keep on building new business opportunities, while people who don't network keep on working for those who build networks.

Robert Kiyosaki, the author of Rich Dad, Poor Dad, says, *"The richest people in the world build networks. Everyone else is trained to look for work."* The whole universe works on the principle of inter-dependence (not independence). Alone, you can work only to a limited extent. But if you network and collaborate with other people, you immediately multiply your knowledge, experience and skillset, resulting in higher performance and greater results.

Take a genuine interest in people both online and offline. Career success is all about relationships, relationships, relationships. The more connected you are, the better the support you'll get at each step in your career.

How to make networking part of your professional habits:

- While at your workplace, try to find a few minutes every day to interact with people from different departments and teams, of course, not at the cost of affecting your performance.

- Attend conferences or seminars related to your work, and build connections.

- Volunteer to work in groups and teams, so you get a chance to get exposed to a different set of people on a regular basis.

➢ **Focus on Helping Others**

In today's so-called modern world, we have become so transactional in our relationships that the joy of simply giving or helping another soul, without the expectation of anything in return, is gradually being thrown out of the window. Our happiness lies in the happiness of other people. Give them their happiness; you will get your own happiness.

Therefore, the next time you do something good for the benefit of another living being, just do it for the sake of being a better human being. The key is not to become proud and have an inflated ego, but just to do good because it is the right thing to do.

Instead of keeping score of the good we have done for others, remember the good that others did for us, and expect nothing in return. It is always good to give back, minus any expectations, as we have been the recipient of so many good things in life.

CHAPTER 7: KEY TAKEAWAYS

Our substantial waking time is consumed by our work, and in fact, our work defines our identity in the world. Depending on how you pursue your work, you can see your work as only a 'job' or you can take this as a 'career' or even 'calling'.

To generate happiness while you are working, alone or with other people, you should incorporate the habits below into your day-to-day life:

- Be **punctual** at work or for any meeting with other people.
- **Start any communication well.**
- Get into the **state of flow** daily.
- **Unplug completely.**
- Be **coachable.**
- **Network** extensively.
- Focus on **helping others.**

Chapter 8: Habits for Happier Relationships with Family and Friends

****

"You don't need too many people to be happy, just a few real ones who appreciate you for who you are."

~ Wiz Khalifa

Solidifying connections with family, friends and like-minded people is one of the surest ways to lasting happiness. Whatever the pace of technology offers, and although it enables you to connect with millions of people through the power of the internet, it's the real one-to-one connection that matters most.

Technology can never provoke the emotions of happiness, joy, or the level of empathy that can be expressed or received from a physical one-to-one meeting with another person over a cup of coffee. Can you experience the love of a child over a Skype call with the same intimacy as you do while you hug and personally see her? Never.

Technology can definitely supplement and make life a bit easier. If you are far away from family, not having an instant mode of communication like phone or video calling and waiting for three days to let your letter reach to your loved ones is definitely unthinkable, so today, we need technology; but we can't use it to replace our physical connections. Sitting over a drink or coffee and having a great laugh for hours can never equate to having 300 Facebook friends who just are your online friends.

In the previous chapter, we already learned about how connection and a sense of belonging are the most important factors for lasting happiness. In this section, we will talk about nurturing those personal relationships with our family, friends and loved ones by building some great habits around them.

➢ Spend Quality Time with Each Other

Bronnie Ware, an Australian nurse, spent many years working in palliative care, caring for patients in the last 12 weeks of their lives. She recorded their dying realizations in a book called *The Top Five Regrets of the Dying*. Not staying in touch with friends was one of the top five regrets of these patients.

Multiple studies have been conducted which prove that quality time spent with friends and family makes a huge difference in upping our happiness quotient. According to Harvard Professor Daniel Gilbert, "We are happy when we have family, we are happy when we have friends, and almost all the other things that we think make us happy are actually just ways of getting more family and friends.[20]"

George E. Vaillant, a leading psychoanalyst and research psychiatrist and a professor at Harvard University, directed a 72-year study of the lives of 268 men. During this study, he observed that the only thing that truly mattered in our lives is our relationships with other people.

A prime example of the link between a person's social connections and overall happiness is close relationships between siblings. An amazing 93% of the men who were in a very happy state of mind at the age of 65 had a close relationship with a sibling when they were younger.

- **Learn Something New and Do Things Together**

Learning new things can be great fun, cultivates closeness and allows us to spend quality time

[20] https://www.yourefirednh.com/why-its-important-to-spend-more-time-with-friends-and-family/

together with our loved ones. Examples are dancing, drawing, pilates, yoga, and sports, to name just a few. Spending quality time with family and friends is not only priceless, but also a great way to bond with each other.

There are so many fun things to engage in, such as playing board games, watching movies, bowling, playing baseball, among the many, many activities we can participate in. Also, we should surprise each other occasionally, for example, taking the children to a theme park, taking your spouse on a sudden getaway, or writing a love letter to them (so rare in today's digital age, yet so personal and heartwarming for your spouse).

- **Be There For One Another and Be Honest With Each Other**

We all make mistakes, and that is to be expected. But we should be confident that we can share our failures and fears with a friend and know they will not judge us or run us down. After all, we all do things that we are not proud of, or even worse, deeply ashamed of. At such times, we certainly don't need to be lectured about how pathetic we are, and about the lack of moral compass within us.

Having a friend who can help us realize our mistake by being a sounding board, without judging us, can help us to come to terms with our internal conflict, which arises when we do things that are less than what was expected of us, is an invaluable blessing. When we need to resolve an issue or require help in improving our behavior, we need a loving, objective and honest assessment from an outsider.

Being able to work through that process with someone who won't judge us is priceless. Everyone deserves a friend who helps us grow as a person and manage their stress in a better way. As it is done out of love and genuine concern, it further reinforces the bond between the two friends.

➢ Appreciate Each Other and Be Grateful

As mentioned earlier, gratitude is what makes life worth living. Without gratitude, it is virtually impossible to attract both abundance and happiness in our lives.

We all are unique in our own ways. God gave us unique talents, and we all possess some good qualities. Rather than criticizing each other and looking for faults, we should encourage and appreciate the positive traits in others. Of course, as mentioned earlier, we should give constructive suggestions that help the other person. This is true both in our personal, as well as professional lives. The key is to give feedback directly to the recipient once we have built that kind of rapport and comfort level.

Alternatively, the feedback can be communicated to the person through someone who he/she is comfortable receiving feedback from. One caution: do not give unsolicited advice to someone who is not receptive to feedback; it could backfire and give exactly the opposite result. Best of all, instead of looking for faults in others, let us look within and find faults within us. When we constantly criticize others, the journey to self-discovery and self-improvement comes to a halt.

For example, if we're driving, it is of utmost importance to concentrate on our driving, so we can navigate the road ahead. However, instead of this, we start focusing on how others are driving and completely forget about our driving. To do that, we have to completely stop driving, which is not possible, as we need to continue moving. In that case, it's just a matter of time before we have an accident.

The same is true of life — we need to continue living. However, if all we do is concentrate on the faults of others, without making an effort at serious introspection and inward growth, we are certain to have some really bad accidents on the road of life. So, why don't we just keep it simple and concentrate on improving ourselves?

- **Don't Judge Others**

If we're not in a position of authority or responsibility, where we are accountable for the growth of a person, such as a parent, do not judge the other person.

Even when coaching or counselling, say, a child, we should adopt the position of a mentor, rather than a stern judge. We should exercise control and inculcate values while giving just the right amount of freedom for children to make mistakes and learn for themselves. No one ever learnt to run without walking, and then falling, while learning how to run. Let them ask questions.

As for the relationships where we have no authority, it is best just to let go and not go out of our way to look for faults. It is best to judge ourselves, so we can improve and grow, because we ourselves are the only persons who we have any degree of control over.

Let go of disappointments and resentment. Holding on to grudges and hatred doesn't hurt the other person, but instead, prevents us from growing and evolving as human beings. In the end, we end up harming ourselves and nobody else.

Life isn't always fair! When we let go, we can see the world with a light head and a fresh perspective, instead of the cobwebs that resentment and hatred bring with them.

Whenever we feel hatred towards someone else, remember the times we offended others, with our thoughts, speech, and actions and were forgiven!

Forgiveness breaks the cycle of action and reaction and leads to a calm mind and a better world. It is critical to cultivate this habit for our own personal growth. No human being is perfect, including us. People will make mistakes; we should show the same large-heartedness and forgiveness that we expect from others when we make mistakes.

- **Keep in Touch**

It is really that simple and basic. Out of sight could well mean out of mind.

If one lives in the same city, it is better to meet regularly, especially with close family and friends, and forge real relationships. If you live in different cities, it is good to visit each other every once in a while. And, one can always call and message each other. And of course, there's social media to keep in touch, provided that it doesn't take over our lives at the cost of real, offline relationships.

How about a heart-to-heart letter, every once in a while, to evoke a sense of nostalgia? A word of caution: it takes two to tango. In the case of a one-sided relationship, when the other person does not reciprocate, it is time to gracefully part ways and move on. We should cultivate new friendships and re-kindle old friendships when the other party is also willing to put in the effort in the relationship.

CHAPTER 8: KEY TAKEAWAYS

Solidifying connections with family, friends, and like-minded people is the surest way to lasting happiness. Loneliness and social isolation lead to poor physical and mental health.

Here is how you can bring happiness by strengthening your relationship with family and friends.

- **Spend quality time** with each other.
- **Learn something new,** and do it together.
- **Be honest** with each other.
- **Appreciate** each other and be grateful.
- **Don't judge** others
- **Keep in touch**.

Chapter 9: 4 Pillars for Unconditional Happiness

****

"Everyone wants to live on top of the mountain, but all the happiness and growth occurs while you're climbing it."

- Andy Rooney

Most people think that happiness is possible only on the happening of certain events and not before.

You must have heard statements like the ones below from others, and you might have found yourself thinking these thoughts:

- I'll be happy when I possess a big house.
- I'll be happy when I drive a luxury car.
- I'll be happy when I find a perfect life partner
- I'll be happy when I have a million dollars in my bank account.
- I'll be happy when I get my hands on the latest version of the iPhone.

What's common in all the above statements? In all such cases, we defer our happiness to the happening of some event or certain material possession. We mistakenly think that once this or that thing happens, we won't have any further desire. Standing here and looking at the future, we think that we will be totally satisfied once we reach there. But we fail to realize that when we achieve our so-called happiness destination, then we start to see a further destination of happiness. It's like a mirage. Once you reach a certain point, you start to look at something more.

Here is the problem with this approach: it's definitely wonderful to think big and go after big goals. There is nothing wrong with that. But when we tie our happiness with the happening of those events, we put ourselves into a vicious circle because we set conditions for our happiness. The best scenario to have is (a) getting excited and thriving to achieve the goal, but at the same time, (b) we need to be joyful in the journey.

Let's understand our life using the metaphor of driving a car. When you go on a long journey, you very well know that you have to keep driving the car to reach there. Now, while driving the car, it's your choice to either keep complaining about the duration of the trip, the quality of roads, or other external circumstances. Or, you can simply focus on driving with a smile on your face, with a belief in your driving abilities, and a faith that you'll reach your destination if you keep driving.

Life is like a journey. The only difference is that the journey of life is for years (not hours). Also, in a driving journey, you always have full confidence in your driving abilities and almost a level of certainty that you'll reach there, despite knowing that many people who leave their homes with a sense of certainty of returning home lose their lives in road accidents. But that doesn't stop you from driving, nor does that make you stressed or anxious about the journey.

But we don't take our lives like driving our car. In the journey of life, instead of enjoying the moments of travel and handling the struggle with a smile on your face, we keep worrying all the time about something wrong happening on the way or just ruminating about the wrong actions that we took in the past.

Also, we keep on doubting our abilities, and we don't maintain faith in life. We think that only when we reach our self-created destination (be it a big house or a big car or a particular amount of money), we will become happier. But we don't realize that at that point in time, there will be another set of problems coming in our way, which we can't foresee as of now.

So, what should we do? I believe that our objective should be attaining the level of happiness that's unconditional.

> ***"I am determined to be cheerful and happy in whatever situation I may find myself. For I have learned that the greater part of our misery or unhappiness is determined not by our circumstance but by our disposition."***
>
> ***~Martha Washington***

Unconditional happiness is something that should be our ultimate goal because then you can control it on your own. You can be happy right here and now. You don't need any big material possessions or other people or any other conditions to become happy. You can just become happier in the present moment. Being happy in no manner means no being sincere or serious about your goals; being happy increases your chances of achieving your goals.

Here are the four pillars that can make your happiness unconditional:

1. **Belief in yourself/your abilities**

Let's start with **ABC Model** from Martin Seligman. It means how beliefs (B) about adversity (A)—and not the adversity itself—cause the consequent (C) feelings. In other words, emotions don't follow inexorably from external events, but from what you *think* about those events, and you can actually change what you think.

Whatever emotions of stress and anxiety we feel, it's due to our belief about how the situation will become adverse, instead of actual adversity. Therefore, we need to work on improving the quality of our beliefs. Belief is not merely a vital part of any major accomplishment; rather, belief is EVERYTHING before you take even the first step in any direction.

You will not commit to any action until you have a strong belief in your mind that it's possible for you. Take any example in your life. Until you believed in the possibility of any goal for you, you didn't take any action. This belief generates a deeper knowing that the goal is possible for you – it generates a sense of certainty of outcome in your mind.

Therefore, you need to develop a strong belief in yourself and your abilities. You can develop any belief by consistently thinking about it and not listening to any naysayers.

"Just believe in yourself. Even if you don't, pretend that you do and, at some point, you will."

~ Venus Williams

If you know what you want to achieve as your goal, and you have belief in yourself and your ability to achieve that goal, it's only a matter of time that you'll achieve what you want. Therefore, a strong belief in yourself sets the solid foundation for inviting happiness that's not dependent upon happening of any events.

2. Develop a Growth Mindset

Another important factor that goes hand in hand with building that strong belief is developing a growth mindset. Carol Dweck, a researcher and psychologist, defines two types of mindsets:

- Fixed mindset
- Growth mindset

Let's understand what they are and how to develop a growth mindset.

In a **fixed mindset**, people believe that their intelligence or other mental abilities are fixed traits and, therefore, cannot change. These people strongly believe that their intelligence and talents are already carved in stone, rather than working to develop and improve them. They also believe that talent alone leads to success, and that significant effort is thus not required.

A fixed-mindset person thinks that if something is difficult and he/she is required to put some effort into it, he/she does not have that talent or capability. Having to put effort into something means it's already a failure.

Alternatively, in a **growth mindset**, people have an underlying belief that their learning and intelligence can grow with time and experience. When people with such a mindset believe they can get smarter, they realize that their effort has an effect on their success, so they put in extra time, leading to higher achievement.

The good news is anyone can develop a growth mindset, thanks to the power of neuroplasticity. Neuroplasticity is the ability of your brain to reorganize itself, both physically and functionally, throughout your life due to changes in your environment, behavior, thinking, and emotions.

Science has shown that neuroplastic changes happen in our entire lives, regardless of age or any other factor. Radical improvements in cognitive function—how we learn, think, perceive, and remember—are possible, even in the elderly. **Your brain makes physical**

changes based on the repetitive things you do and the experiences that you have.

If you want to develop a growth mindset, the easiest solution is to associate with the right kind of people, go to resourceful events, and expose your mind to new things on a consistent basis. The growth mindset will further bolster your belief that you can learn anything towards your journey to achieving your goals. Also, you will consider failure as a stepping-stone to success. The combination of strong belief about yourself and having a growth mindset makes you immune to any kind of negative thinking. You just focus on what matters, and this puts you into a state of flow.

3. Unwavering Faith or Certainty of Outcome

What is faith?

The dictionary meaning of Faith[21] is "a *firm belief in something for which there is no proof*" or "*something that is believed especially with strong conviction.*"

The world's top-most strategic coach, Tony Robbins, puts it differently, as the "certainty of outcome" in your mind at the stage you start working towards your goals. He states that our success in any venture we get into entirely

[21] https://www.merriam-webster.com/dictionary/faith

depends on the level of certainty of outcome in our minds because only our thinking about the certainty of the outcome will trigger us to produce the quality of actions needed to get the results.

> ***"Faith is taking the first step, even if you don't see the whole staircase." ~ Martin Luther King, Jr.***

With a strong belief in our abilities and a growth mindset, additionally, we need to develop a deeper sense of complete faith in the goodness of whatever happens in our life. Of course, it doesn't mean that when you have faith or believe strongly in the certainty of the outcome you expect, you'll always achieve what you desire. There are many uncontrollable factors that play a significant role, so despite your best efforts, you won't get the results as desired.

But failures won't steal your happiness because you are already equipped with a growth mindset. Failure gives you the required experience and prompts you to develop the skill set necessary to handle the situation better.

Having faith means that even if things don't go the way you desired, you believe in the bigger scheme of things — you believe in the unfolding of life towards a greater good for you. When you have faith, you strongly believe that things don't happen to you; they happen for you.

> ***"Remember that sometimes, not getting what you want is a wonderful stroke of luck." ~ Dalai Lama***

---

4. **Consistent Action**

With all the above three weapons in our armoury, we can't stop taking consistent action towards what we desire.

You know that you can't control your genes or circumstances, but you can control your actions. You also realize that as you don't have full control over everything, so you are mindful that your happiness shouldn't depend on the outcome. Your happiness comes from taking action and getting immersed in the activities rather than overthinking about the past or future. When you take consistent and massive action, you invite flow in your work, and your happiness is created by your immersion into the activities.

So instead of waiting for some outcome to happen to make you happier, you immediately experience happiness in the work you do. And I'd say it's a win-win proposition. Because if you are joyful and get into flow in whatever you do, there are great chances that the quality of your work will be multiple times better than when you are stressed.

The combination of these four elements leaves no room for stress in the present moment, as you don't stop taking action because you have a growth mindset, so you are ready to learn and grow. You believe in yourself and have faith in the unfolding of the events.

In the end, the objective of life is to strive for our goals, because growth is the need of our spirit, but at the same time, we need to ensure that we don't tie our momentary happiness on the achievement of those goals.

Eleanor Roosevelt once said, ***"Do not stop thinking of life as an adventure."*** If you think life as an adventure, you'll enjoy all the challenges coming in the way. Instead of avoiding, you'll move forward to seek those challenges.

CHAPTER 10: KEY TAKEAWAYS

Our happiness shouldn't depend on the occurrence of any outside events. If you're stuck in beliefs like "I'll be happy when... (i.e. on happening of any event or acquiring any possessions), you need to RESET your beliefs. Beliefs play a vital role in building unconditional happiness.

The **ABC Model** tells us that how beliefs (B) about adversity (A)—and not the adversity itself—cause the consequent (C) feelings.

If you want to develop unconditional happiness in your life, regardless of outside circumstances, here are the **four pillars** that will strengthen your foundational work for that.

- Strengthen **belief** in yourself and your abilities.

- Develop a **growth mindset**: Change your environment and use the power of neuroplasticity to develop a growth mindset.

- Unshakeable **faith**: Develop a sense of certainty of outcome. Even if things don't turn out the way you wanted, believe that there is something better waiting for you.

- Consistent **action**: By taking consistent and massive action towards your goals, you build engagement and invite 'flow' in your work, and that gives you instant happiness.

Conclusion

****

"Happiness is not something you postpone for the future; it is something you design for the present."

~ Jim Rohn

Congratulations! You have come to the end of this book. A vast majority of the readers don't finish the book, but you did, so you deserve a pat on your back. I hope it was a good journey and hope you have a smile on your face as you are reading this final page of the book. After all, I was trying to build a happier brain throughout this book.

You have now read and understood the psychology and neuroscience of happiness. You now know how to disengage with your thoughts and emotions and give them a direction. You also know that habits are the solid foundation upon which we can construct the building of happiness. You have found the simple but effective habits that can create new neural pathways in your mind, and you'll be able to make better decisions and take better actions with your happier brain now.

You already know that habits put our actions on autopilot mode and keep us organized. A disorganized person finds it difficult to honor commitments, even if it means something as basic as being on time for a meeting. In conclusion, habits give us a sense of discipline and a framework to manage our lives and our time.

When practiced consistently and thoroughly, they bring out the best in us, by making us utilize time effectively. Especially in today's fast-paced, high-stress life, time is the greatest asset one has. Remember, time is the stuff life's made of.

So, I hope you would commit yourself to practice at least a few of the habits every day.

As people say, knowledge is power, but the truth is that merely getting knowledge doesn't move the needle. Knowledge is potential power. It becomes really powerful when bolstered with the power of consistent action.

Now, I would urge you to take action, follow the habits, and build a happier brain. I'm sure they will lead to a life of abundance, joy, and lasting happiness.

I wish you a splendid life full of happiness and fulfilment.

Cheers

May I ask you for a small favor?

At the outset, I want to give you a big thanks for taking out time to read this book. You could have chosen any other book, but you took mine, and I totally appreciate this.

I hope you got at least a few actionable insights that will have a positive impact on your day to day life.

Can I ask for 30 seconds more of your time?

I'd love if you could leave a review about the book. Reviews may not matter to big-name authors; but they're a tremendous help for authors like me, who don't have much following. They help me to grow my readership by encouraging folks to take a chance on my books.

To put it straight– **reviews are the life blood for any author.**

Please leave your review by clicking below link, it will directly lead you to book review page.

DIRECT REVIEW LINK FOR "BUILD A HAPPIER BRAIN"

It will just take less than a minute of your time, but will tremendously help me to reach out to more people, so please leave your review.

Thanks for your support to my work. And I'd love to see your review.

Full Book Summary

CHAPTER 1: KEY TAKEAWAYS

Happiness depends on what goes on inside your brain. If you learn to build a happier brain, this will not only **improve your physical and mental health**; you'll also attain more **financial success** and a **rewarding career**.

Happiness is your **life currency**, just like money is the currency for any business. Your primary objective should be to enhance your levels of happiness while pursuing your goals. Your happiness need not depend on outside events. You can **choose to create happiness** in your life, but you have to put in the work.

It demands making little difficult and permanent changes that require effort and commitment every day of your life. It **takes work to pursue the journey of happiness**, but consider that this happiness work may be the most rewarding work that you'll ever do for a richer and rewarding life.

CHAPTER 2: KEY TAKEAWAYS

Of course, money plays a significant role in bringing happiness into your life; but you commit a big mistake when you attribute money as a sole factor to happiness. Other than a lack of money, there are many reasons why most people are not happy today. Here are some of the most common reasons.

- **Needless comparison** with others without knowing their journey: If you are not willing to pay the price what others have paid, don't compare; you'll only invite unhappiness.

- Maintaining an **artificial online persona**: Living an inauthentic life will bring you more stress.

- Association with **negative people**: They suck all the energy and happiness out of you.

- Continuously **regretting your past**: You can't drive your car fast if you keep looking in the rear-view mirror.

- **Lack of family and friends**: Humans are designed to thrive in communities with others. Social isolation can also cause illness.

- Seeing the world through your **own narrow prism**: No man is an island; expand your horizon by understanding others' perspectives.

- **Lack of gratitude**: If you are not grateful for what you have, what's the probability of becoming happier when you get more? Savour what you have while striving for what you want.

CHAPTER 3: KEY TAKEAWAYS

Success without fulfillment is the ultimate failure.

There are two broad aspects or concepts of happiness: **Hedonia** (i.e. all about maximized emotions of pleasure and minimized pain) and **Eudaimonia** (i.e. happiness is a result of the development and expression of individual strengths and virtues).

Instead of focusing solely on the pleasures of life, we need to also focus on leaving a life of meaning.

Martin Seligman, also known as the father of positive psychology, over a period of time, developed certain theories around happiness and finally concluded with the '**Well-being Theory**" or **PERMA Model**. PERMA is an acronym where each letter describes a factor that plays a vital role in human well-being. It is composed of:

P- Positive Emotions: Feeling good, optimism, pleasure and enjoyment

E- Engagement: Fulfilling work, interesting hobbies, and flow

R- Relationship: Social connection, love, intimacy, emotional and physical connection

M- Meaning: Having a purpose, finding meaning in life

A- Accomplishments: Ambitions, realistic goals, important achievements, pride in yourself

All the elements of the PERMA model play a vital role, and you can significantly improve your life's well-being by focusing on and taking care of all the elements together.

CHAPTER 4: KEY TAKEAWAYS

Human behavior is primarily governed by an individual's physiological and psychological needs. Human desires or needs drive individuals to act and behave differently at various stages of life to become happier.

I. Maslow's Hierarchy of Needs

Abraham Maslow, an American psychologist, developed a need theory where he explained how there is a hierarchy to human needs, starting with basic physical needs and ascending to higher intellectual needs. Here is the hierarchy of the six human needs that become the key motivator for happiness at different stages of one's life:

- **Physiological Needs**: related to the survival of the human body, food, shelter, clothing, i.e. basic life necessities
- **Safety Needs**: safety from war, natural disaster, economic safety, health-related safety, etc.
- **Love & Belonging**: need for family, friends, and intimate relationship with someone
- **Esteem**: concern with getting recognition, status, importance, and respect from others
- **Self-Actualization**: the desire to accomplish everything that one can, to become the most one can be
- **Self-Transcendence**: craving for contribution to the world that transcends beyond yourself

II. Inherent Psychological Needs:

Under the Self-Determination Theory, the last level of happiness requires intrinsic motivation, and it is characterized by three innate psychological needs that give us lasting happiness. They are:

- The need for **Human Connection**
- The need for **Mastery**: to be efficacious in whatever once chooses as a career
- The need for **Autonomy**: to not be controlled by anyone and to be able to make decisions independently

III. The Six Core Needs for Fulfillment

Tony Robbins has categorized the human needs to attain fulfillment in two different baskets (1) the four needs of our personality; and (2) the two needs of our spirit, as described below:

- **Certainty**: the need for safety, comfort and consistency
- **Uncertainty**: the need for variety or novelty in life.
- **Significance**: the need to be acknowledged and recognized for what you do
- **Love and Belonging**: the need to both love and be loved by others and to have a sense of belonging

- **Growth**: growth at all levels, including **physical, emotional, mental and spiritual**
- **Contribution**: desire to give meaning to our lives by making a difference to the world.

CHAPTER 5: KEY TAKEAWAYS

Our brain is one of the most complex and sophisticated chemical factories on the planet. Behind all our emotions, be they happiness, sadness, love, greed, anger, there is an interplay between multiple chemicals happening inside our brains.

To consistently experience feelings of happiness, we need to find out the ways and ensure that we trigger the release of four primary chemicals in our brain. Commonly stated as an acronym, DOSE, these four chemicals, when released, make us happier.

- **D**opamine: triggered by anticipation and inspires us to take action towards goals.
- **O**xytocin: a feeling of human connectedness; you can release more by hugging your loved ones or shaking hands.

- **S**erotonin: leads to feeling significant; try to recall past achievements to release this.
- **E**ndorphins: helps us to fight pain; exercise, on a regular basis, releases more endorphins.

In a nutshell, for a daily D.O.S.E. of happiness, engage in the following activities:

- Exercise (e.g. run, walk)
- Laugh/cry
- Hug and/or shake hands with your friends
- Anticipate something good. Book your mini-vacation, maybe just a small weekend. When you are anticipating something, you are happier.
- Set and achieve goals
- Build social connections. Appreciate others for their good work. Accept accountability for certain activities, and enjoy being acknowledged.

CHAPTER 6: KEY TAKEAWAYS

Self-awareness is the key to taking control of your mind. The way to self-awareness is getting disengaged from your thoughts and emotions.

To experience happiness on a consistent basis requires a deeper sense of awareness.

The following habits will help you disengage with your mind as well as build happiness in your personal life:

- Practice **Gratitude**
- **Breathe** deeply
- **Exercise** regularly
- **Empty your head** through journaling
- Practice **Mindfulness**
- **Surround yourself** with quality people
- Do some **random act of kindness** daily

The best part is that you don't need a great deal of time to inculcate these habits in your daily life.

Assuming you are too busy, still if you could just spare just half an hour, you can instil above habits in your daily routine. To be specific, practicing gratitude shouldn't take more than 2 minutes, journaling can be done in 5 minutes, breathing and mindfulness practices can be done in under 15 minutes. You can do intensive exercise for 10 minutes every day, and do a bit more over the weekend.

And this additional half an hour can be generated by sleeping and thus waking up 30 minutes earlier. Maybe you can cut down some time out of other activities that take your time in the morning or in the evening.

Even half hour of regular practice will start to reward you in the form of higher self-awareness, reduced stress, and bring more calm and joy in your life, in a matter of few weeks.

CHAPTER 7: KEY TAKEAWAYS

Our substantial waking time is consumed by our work, and in fact, our work defines our identity in the world. Depending on how you pursue your work, you can see your work as only a 'job' or you can take this as a 'career' or even 'calling'.

To generate happiness while you are working, alone or with other people, you should incorporate the habits below into your day-to-day life:

- Be **punctual** at work or for any meeting with other people.
- **Start any communication well.**
- Get into the **state of flow** daily.
- **Unplug completely.**
- Be **coachable.**
- **Network** extensively.
- Focus on **helping others.**

CHAPTER 8: KEY TAKEAWAYS

Solidifying connections with family, friends, and like-minded people is the surest way to lasting happiness. Loneliness and social isolation lead to poor physical and mental health.

Here is how you can bring happiness by strengthening your relationship with family and friends.

- **Spend quality time** with each other.
- **Learn something new,** and do it together.
- **Be honest** with each other.
- **Appreciate** each other and be grateful.
- **Don't judge** others
- **Keep in touch**.

CHAPTER 10: KEY TAKEAWAYS

Our happiness shouldn't depend on the occurrence of any outside events. If you're stuck in beliefs like "I'll be happy when... (i.e. on happening of any event or acquiring any possessions), you need to RESET your beliefs. Beliefs play a vital role in building unconditional happiness.

The **ABC Model** tells us that how beliefs (B) about adversity (A)—and not the adversity itself—cause the consequent (C) feelings.

If you want to develop unconditional happiness in your life, regardless of outside circumstances, here are the **four pillars** that will strengthen your foundational work for that.

- Strengthen **belief** in yourself and your abilities.

- Develop a **growth mindset**: Change your environment and use the power of neuroplasticity to develop a growth mindset.

- Unshakeable **faith**: Develop a sense of certainty of outcome. Even if things don't turn out the way you wanted, believe that there is something better waiting for you.

- Consistent **action**: By taking consistent and massive action towards your goals, you build engagement and invite 'flow' in your work, and that gives you instant happiness.

Could you please leave a review on the book?

One last time!

I'd love if you could leave a review about the book. Reviews may not matter to big-name authors; but they're a tremendous help for authors like me, who don't have much following. They help me to grow my readership by encouraging folks to take a chance on my books.

To put it straight– **reviews are the life blood for any author.**

Please leave your review by clicking below link, it will directly lead you to book review page.

DIRECT REVIEW LINK FOR "BUILD A HAPPIER BRAIN"

It will just take less than a minute of yours, but will tremendously help me to reach out to more people, so please leave your review.

Thank you for supporting my work and I'd love to see your review on the book.

Preview of the book "Think With Full Brain"

Introduction

****

"One of the saddest experiences that can ever happen to a human being is to awaken gray-haired and wrinkled, near the close of a very unproductive career, to the fact that all through the past years, he has been using only a small part of himself."

—Orison Swett Marden

A Quick Story

One day, a professor entered his classroom and asked his students to prepare for a surprise exam. They all waited anxiously at their desks for the exam to begin.

The professor handed out the test papers to students with the text facing down. After he disseminated them all out, he asked the students to turn over the papers.

To everyone's surprise, there were no questions – just a black dot in the center of the paper. Obviously, the students were confused about how to deal with this surprise test. The professor, seeing the expression on everyone's faces, told them:

"I want you to write about what you see on the test paper."

The students were still confused, but they started on the mysterious task.

At the end of the class, the professor took all the answer sheets and started reading each one of them out loud in front of all the students. All of them, with no exception, defined the black dot – some tried to explain its position in the center of the sheet, while others described its size; a few others talked about the color of the dot. But every answer targeted the black dot.

After all the answers were read, the classroom was silent, waiting for the right answer to the confusing surprise test. Now the professor started to explain. He expressed:

"I'm not going to grade you on this; I just wanted to give you something to think about. No one wrote about the white part of the paper. Everyone focused on the black dot – and the same thing happens in our lives. We insist on focusing only on the black dot.

The black dot is an allegory; it represents the problems that you face in any area of your life, be they health issues, lack of money, a complicated relationship, or frustration caused by a stressful career. But we get so wrapped up in the black dot (our problems) that we miss out on the bigger context. By focusing too much on a problem, we often limit our thinking and are not able to seek out solutions that are readily available to us.

This is especially interesting when you consider how the black dot is tiny relative to the amount of white space it is surrounded by. If you start looking beyond the black dot and broaden your thinking to reflect on your problem (the black dot) in the context of the surrounding possibilities and solutions (the white space), you might start to get a glimpse of solutions in the form of resourceful people who may be able to assist you, opportunities in nearby areas, or skills that you may be overlooking due to your tunnel vision with regards to your problem.

And what is the moral of the story? The original message was that one should not only look at the dark side but also focus on the white space, i.e. the brighter side of the things. But as a thought experiment, I wondered what other lessons this story could offer, and, to my mind, this story perfectly addresses the concept of holistic thinking as well.

This anecdote also reminds me of the famous fictional character, Sherlock Holmes, created by Arthur Canon Doyle., who often proclaims this insight while investigating any complex case, **“people see but don’t observe”.** You see the difference. While seeing is limiting oneself to only looking at the black dot, on the other hand, observing is equivalent to grasping the whole context of the black dot relative to the white space. Observing is analyzing the problem in its context by looking at the surrounding objects and people and examining the interrelation between them.

Now, let’s depart the fictional universe and get into the real world. Our thinking is developed based on our routines and patterns, which are significantly influenced by our family background, our society, and the environment we spend most of our time in. In fact, our pattern of thinking and our perspective change heavily under the influence of the culture and geographies we belong to.

How Culture and Geography Changes the Way We Think

A few research studies have shown that East Asians are culturally more likely to explain any event or problem with reference to its context than Americans, who are focused solely on issues or problems in isolation. Two specific studies compare the context-sensitivity of Japanese and Americans and explain how thinking and behavior changes based on geography and culture.

Psychologists Richard E. Nisbett and Takahiko Masuda, from the University of Michigan, conducted an experiment,[22] wherein they presented a 20-second animated video of underwater scenes to two different groups comprising Japanese and American participants respectively. Afterward, participants were asked what they had seen.

Here is how both groups responded:

While the Americans mentioned larger, faster-moving, brightly-colored objects in the foreground (such as the big fish), the Japanese described more about what was going on in the background (for example, the small frog at the bottom left). Interestingly, it was also noted that the Japanese also spoke twice as often as the Americans about the interdependencies between the objects in the front and the objects in the background. Japanese were more context-specific and viewed the whole event with a holistic approach.

---

22 https://sites.ualberta.ca/~tmasuda/index.files/Masuda&Nisbett2001.pdf

Similarly, in another experiment, two groups, one American and one Japanese, were asked to take a picture of one individual. The results found that the American people frequently zoomed in on the picture in order to view the intricate facial features in greater detail. On the other hand, the Japanese, when asked to click a picture, frequently took pictures with wider coverage that showed the complete individual from head to toe, as well as objects surrounding that individual such as bookshelves, chairs, floors, etc.

One can readily see the similarities between both studies. The Americans focused on individual items isolated from their backgrounds and contexts, while the Asians gave more attention to the backgrounds and to the interaction or contextual relationship between these backgrounds and the central figures. Why do these two groups approach these situational experiments with such vastly different perspectives?

Erin Meyer, a professor at INSEAD, where she heads the executive education program on leading across borders and cultures, explains the reasoning behind it. She states that a traditional tenet of Western philosophies and religions is that you can remove an item from its environment and analyze it separately. Cultural theorists call this ***specific thinking***. Chinese religions and philosophies, by contrast, have traditionally emphasized interdependencies and interconnectedness. The Ancient Chinese used the ***holistic thinking*** approach, believing that action always occurs in a field of forces. You can't disregard the environmental forces behind any action.

In fact, the Chinese have a concept of *yin* and *yang* in ancient Chinese philosophy that describes how seemingly opposite or contrary forces may actually be complementary, interconnected, and interdependent in the natural world, and how they may give rise to each other as they interrelate to one another.

Why did I start the book with these two studies?

I did not intend to compare any specific cultures or geographies or leave any positive or adverse comments on any specific set of the population. The idea is to simply communicate that when two people are dealing with or talking to each other in any context, in most cases, they make judgments about other people and label them right or wrong. They wrongly believe that the other person is not perceiving the information correctly. But what they miss out on is that there could be many perspectives or approaches of examining things, depending on their geography, culture, societal values, and upbringing.

What if you could understand all these perspectives while interacting with people?

What if you could hear what they are saying in some particular context? What if you could also see what they are seeing?

Imagine, if you could, how different and exciting your life would be. It would be a journey full of exploration and adventure because every other person will show you their own perception or view about something that is different from what you think and believe. Every day, every meeting, and every interaction with another person will offer you diverse approaches of looking at things.

If that happens, you'll start making clear distinctions in your mind about why different people think differently and alter your perspective about things, places, situations, and people. You'll view things in a more holistic manner and offer better solutions.

Does that sound interesting?

That's what we will cover here: how to start thinking with your full brain.

Why Think with Your Full Brain?

Neuroscience has progressed enough, and there are many non-invasive brain-testing technologies these days like fMRI (functional magnetic resonance imaging) that can see inside of the human brain and have already figured out the inner constituents of our brain.

Robert Sperry's split-brain research that won him the Nobel Prize in medicine proved that the human brain has two hemispheres, right and left. Each side of the brain thinks in a different pattern. While the left side of the brain deals with rational and logical thought processes, the right side of the brain is inclined towards imagination, intuition, and interpersonal human aspects of thinking.

We are talking about thinking with our whole brains, so obviously, we will not get into a debate about which hemisphere is better or worse. The objective here is to use the full potential of your brain to make holistic and better decisions in most life situations.

In fact, people tend to use one side of their brains dominantly, just like people use one hand as their dominant hand while performing their regular tasks.

But you can't and shouldn't be solely relying on one particular segment of the brain to do all of your mental work. Let's set the research and proof aside for a moment and consider this statement with a logical perspective only. Why is a human being created with two brain hemispheres if they are not both useful and essential to one's life? Can you look at your outer body and say that any part of your body is inessential? Or can you just feel the sensations or vibrations inside your body and conclude that few organs of our inner system are inessential?

No body part or organ of your body is inessential. Every outside part or internal organ of the body has some role to play. So why would you prefer to use only one part or to restrict the usage of the other part of your most precious treasure – your brain? You should be using all the areas of the brain to their fullest potential...

Both hemispheres of our brain have specific roles to play, and we will examine these roles later in much greater detail. There is nothing bad about having a specific preference for one hemisphere or the other, but that shouldn't mean that you should be neglecting the other important aspects of your thinking brain. You can think with your entire brain capacity and still maintain a preference for one area of thinking, and that will make you a holistic thinker.

Neuroanatomist Jill Bolte Taylor describes the two hemispheres and how they work together in her book, *My Stroke of Insight*: "Although each of our cerebral hemispheres processes information in uniquely different ways, the two work intimately together when it comes to just about every action we take. **The more we understand about how our hemispheres work together to create our perception of reality, the more successful we will be in**

understanding the natural gifts of our own brains."

Here are a few of the benefits that you will reap from thinking with your full brain:

- **A heightened level of awareness**: You will appreciate everything that's going on around you with a holistic, context-based approach as your powers of perception and imagination increase.

- **Increased entrepreneurial capabilities**: Every business idea requires a lot of creative brainstorming. By thinking with your whole brain, you will be able to transform and integrate an idea (from its inception to actualization) into a business.

- **Faster progress in your career:** By understanding how different parts of your brain work, you will better understand the requirements of your clients, superiors, and organization, and you will be more equipped to meet or exceed their expectations.

- **Better relationships with family and friends**: Thinking with your whole brain enhances your interpersonal skills and emotional intelligence. This, in turn, increases your ability to understand the perspective of your family members, friends, or coworkers. Therefore, you avoid unnecessary arguments, are more open to others' perspectives, and consequently, you have deeper, more fulfilling relationships.

- **The development of multiple forms of intelligence**: Human beings are bestowed with multiple forms of intelligence that most people don't know about. We will cover them later on in this book. When you practice thinking with your whole brain, you become empowered to develop multiple types of intelligence.

Daniel Pink, the bestselling author of *The Whole New Mind*, has rightly said,

"Left brain approaches haven't become obsolete. They've become insufficient. What people need today isn't one side of the brain or the other, but ... a whole new mind."

What Should You Expect From This Book?

The title of this book, *Think with Full Brain,* is based on the premise that most people don't utilize their full brain potential. They employ limited aspects of their thinking abilities and, therefore, don't get the benefit of the ultimate level of self-actualization they are capable of.

I want people to unleash their fullest potential, and that's not possible until they understand their most complex organ: the brain. The objective of this book is to let the readers explore different parts of their brains and understand how thinking works differently in different parts of the brain. You'll learn and understand the dominant area of thinking preference in your brain, as well as where your blind spots are. Then we will explore how to enrich different parts of the brain and their thinking faculties to help you further strengthen your dominant way of thinking and make the other parts of your brain reasonably strong so that you can become situationally whole-brained and understand and handle different life situations in a wiser and more holistic manner.

By the end of this book, you'll realize a significant difference in how you see your own thinking from different aspects and use this knowledge to your advantage. Moreover, you'll also sharpen your brain to understand the other peoples' perspectives and thinking styles and adapt your thinking approach according to whatever situation that you are in.

--End of Preview--

Get your copy of the full book >>> *Think With Full Brain*

Other Books in Power-Up Your Brain Series

1. ***Intelligent Thinking:** Overcome Thinking Errors, Learn Advanced Techniques to Think Intelligently, Make Smarter Choices, and Become the Best Version of Yourself (Power-Up Your Brain Series Book 1)*

2. ***Think Out of The Box:** Generate Ideas on Demand, Improve Problem Solving, Make Better Decisions, and Start Thinking Your Way to the Top (Power-Up Your Brain Series Book 2)*

3. ***Make Smart Choices:** Learn How to Think Clearly, Beat Information Anxiety, Improve Decision Making Skills, and Solve Problems Faster (Power-Up Your Brain Series Book 3)*

4. ***Build A Happier Brain:** The Neuroscience and Psychology of Happiness. Learn Simple Yet Effective Habits for Happiness in Personal,*

Professional Life and Relationships (Power-Up Your Brain Book 4)

5. ***Think With Full Brain:*** *Strengthen Logical Analysis, Invite Breakthrough Ideas, Level-up Interpersonal Intelligence, and Unleash Your Brain's Full Potential (Power-Up Your Brain Series Book 5)*

Printed in Great Britain
by Amazon